Our SAVANNAH

From Ardsley Park to Twickenham and Beyond

POLLY POWERS STRAMM

THE History PRESS

Published by The History Press
Charleston, SC 29403
www.historypress.net

First published 2009

Manufactured in the United States

ISBN 978.1.59629.764.7

Library of Congress Cataloging-in-Publication Data

Stramm, Polly Powers, 1954-
Our Savannah : from Ardsley Park to Twickenham and beyond / Polly Powers Stramm.
p. cm.
ISBN 978-1-59629-764-7
1. Savannah (Ga.)--Social life and customs--20th century--Anecdotes. 2. Savannah (Ga.)--History--20th century--Anecdotes. 3. Neighborhoods--Georgia--Savannah. 4. Savannah (Ga.)--Biography--Anecdotes. I. Title.
F294.S2S75 2009
975.8'724--dc22
2009038808

CONTENTS

Contents

INTRODUCTION AND ACKNOWLEDGEMENTS

Not too long ago, I asked my longtime friend Mary Frances Bright Hendrix to share with me her memories of our neighborhood—an area that we knew like the backs of our hands.

"What I remember most is that there was always someone to play with and we always thought of something to do," she said. "We just hopped on our bikes and started riding to find someone to go with to the [Victory Soda Shop]," she said.

Mary Frances and I are akin to many folks who grew up not just in Savannah, but in most Anywhere, USA. We cherish wonderful memories of the neighborhood in which we lived. I discovered this nostalgic phenomenon during the last two decades while writing my "Polly's People" column for Savannah's daily newspapers.

For some reason, I tend to gravitate toward enthusiastic folks who take tremendous pleasure in regaling me with the fascinating details of what life used to be like. They might entertain me with tales about their neighborhoods and the stores where they shopped. Or they may introduce me—via their recollections—to the friends with whom they shared these unforgettable experiences.

Always, after one of these columns is printed, my mailbox is jammed with notes and letters from readers who thank me for letting them stroll down memory lane. "Keep it up," one man wrote, because "it does us good to remember a more carefree time." Part of an anonymous note that I framed

Polly Powers Stramm (as a teenager) with old friends Greg Odrezin and Mary Frances Bright Hendrix. *Author's collection.*

and put in my office applauds me for continuing "to squeeze as much as you can out of the priceless pieces of local history."

It astounds me that anyone would consider me an expert at anything, especially Savannah's history. I'm simply someone who likes to sit down with folks and listen to their stories. I organize and fine-tune those thoughts and put them in print, trusting that the people who are kind enough to talk with me are as accurate as possible in their memories.

Officially, the city of Savannah lists 108 neighborhoods. The outskirts also are considered part of Savannah, a point that readers will notice in a few of my stories. Space and time didn't permit me to include everyone's neighborhood in this book. Hopefully, though, I will hear from more people who can tell me what life was like when they were growing up in Savannah so I can put together additional books.

With that said, I offer an enthusiastic "thank-you" to everyone who was kind enough to relive their neighborhood memories and share their treasured photographs with me. I also would like to acknowledge the generosity of the editors and management of the *Savannah Morning News* for allowing me to reprint a few of my columns for this book.

THE SUGAR REFINERY

Could Life Have Been Any Sweeter?

Joyce Cooper Johnson insists that she and others who lived in the frame houses once provided for employees of the Savannah Sugar Refinery "couldn't have had a better childhood than we did. We were so well taken care of," she said.

Joyce, who was born in the 1930s, says, "It was a blessing to be living [at the refinery] during the Depression." During difficult economic times, sugar refinery employees agreed to "work a four-day week rather than be laid off."

"What was so neat about [living at the sugar refinery] was that we were like one humongous family," she explained. "We [children] belonged to everybody."

Like many other sugar refinery employees, Joyce's grandfather, Louis Joseph "Papa" Weber, came to Port Wentworth in 1917 from Cajun country in Louisiana to work at the new plant in Savannah. "He couldn't bring his family then because the houses were just being built," she said, adding that he probably stayed in the refinery's two-story "hotel," which was a boardinghouse, until the houses were completed.

Joyce's parents, Wilhelmina Weber and John Walter Cooper Jr., met at a sugar refinery party at the two-story hotel, part of which is still standing. "We used to have all our parties there," she said. "I can remember eating in that kitchen." She won't ever forget hearing the whistle blow at noon "so all the men could go home for dinner."

After the Coopers married, they lived in Savannah, but when Joyce was a toddler, they moved in with Papa, who was a widower, and her two aunts at

Joyce Cooper Johnson and her brother, Johnny Cooper, at the Savannah Sugar Refinery, home of Dixie Crystals Sugar. *Courtesy of Joyce Johnson.*

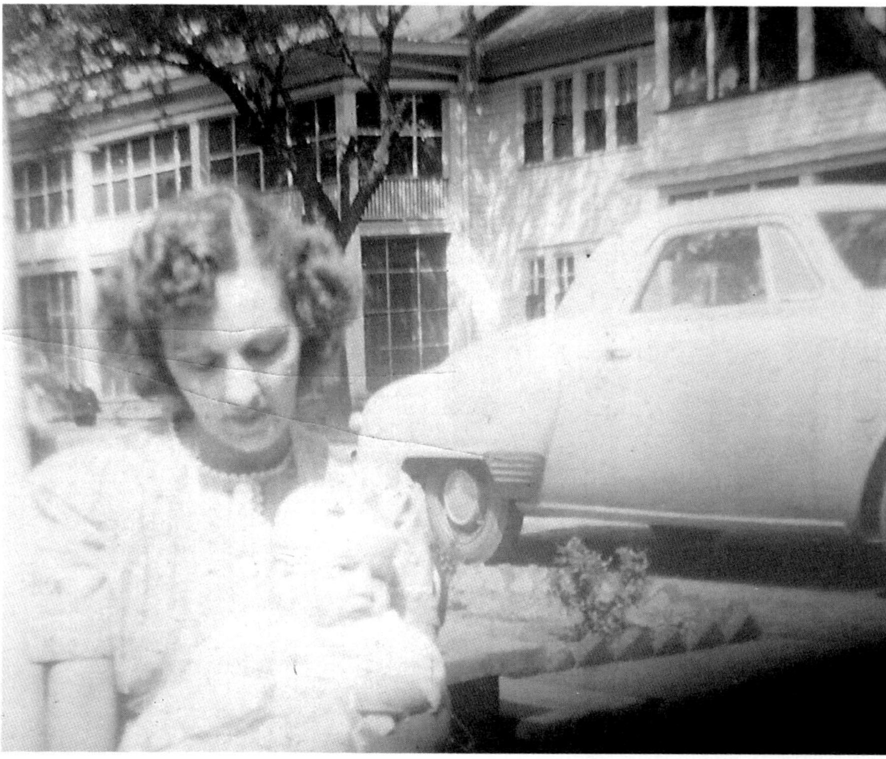

Residents referred to this two-story building at the Savannah Sugar Refinery as the "hotel." *Courtesy of Joyce Johnson.*

the sugar refinery. Joyce's father worked at the shipyard and taught welding at the vocational-technical school.

Employee houses lined two streets on the property, she said. "The streets were called Front Street and Back Street," she added. She and her family lived in a one-story house on Front Street. She also recalls having ducks in her backyard and how her "Daddy and my Papa" would wring the necks of chickens. "I would run in my bedroom and put the pillow over my head," she said.

The village was full of unforgettable characters, like a "precious man" named Johnny Logue. "He looked after all us kids," Joyce explained. Roxie "Mother" Edwards had a cow or two and delivered milk by horse and wagon. It wasn't uncommon for children to call their neighbors "uncle and aunt," she said. "We grew up calling them that."

Joyce's mother could get on the party line and phone in her grocery order to DeReese's store, which was "one big room" with glassed-in counters near

Wilhelmina and John Cooper with their children, John III and Joyce, at the Savannah Sugar Refinery. *Courtesy of Joyce Johnson.*

the sawmill on the Savannah River, Joyce said. A Greek store on refinery property was frequented by Joyce and pals like Dru Grevemberg ("bless her heart, those ducks didn't like her"), Carol Bercegeay, JoAnn Coburn, Delores Niver and Roxie Barras. "Most of us went to school together from the first grade to the twelfth," she said.

After all these years, a couple of sugar refinery traditions still stand out in Joyce's memory. The driveway into the plant—now called Oxnard Drive—was lined with oak trees and gardenia bushes, she said. "When someone died, the body was in the home [for the wake] and everyone brought gardenias," she explained. In the evenings, folks enjoyed leisurely strolls down the driveway to the highway. "We would walk to what we called the car line, which had been the trolley on [Highway 17]," she said.

SAVANNAH'S MOVIE THEATRES

Some Long Gone While Others Remain Treasures

Readers who saw a movie memories column that I once wrote couldn't resist sharing their stories of Savannah's long-ago theatres, or "picture shows," as my neighbor refers to them.

George Smith, for example, was in high school when he managed the Victory Theatre on Bull Street. He recalled:

> *We showed movies "day and date" with the Lucas downtown. That meant while a first-run movie was available at the Lucas, we were showing the same movie at the Victory for those who wanted to come to a less formal place. We had movies at 5:00 p.m., 7:00 p.m. and 9:00 p.m. I can remember getting out of school on the distributive education program—my teacher was Ida Barber—at around noon every day. I would go to the Bijou where the company—Lucas Theatres Group with Hudson Edwards as general manager—stored candy and chewing gum and then over to the Lucas where popcorn was popped en masse for all the theaters in the group. I'd load it all up in the rumble seat of my 1935 Ford coupe and drive it to the Victory for the evening performances.*

George's biggest challenge at the Victory was keeping all the guys from Paul's Soda Shop, just down the street, from trying to get in for free. "Finally, I found it easier to allow them in free just to save our time and effort to prevent otherwise," he said.

Going to the "picture show" back in the day involved dressing up. *Author's collection.*

George also worked as an usher and doorman at the Lucas in the late 1940s and early '50s and remembers the stiff competition between the theatres. George can't forget the Elbow Room inside the Odeon Theatre, where folks could grab a quick burger and soda. He also remembers bargain admission prices—the nine-cent fare at the Odeon and the Roxie. When he and his sister were downtown, they visited Tanner's, where they could buy a sandwich and orange drink along with all the red-skinned peanuts they could eat for about fifteen cents. Even before all of that, George remembers his father taking him and his sister to the Savannah Theatre on Saturday afternoons and sharing those great five-cent bags of popcorn. "We sat in the balcony, for my dad had to snooze while we watched the cartoons, the current serial and then the double feature—a Western, naturally," he recalled.

Leon Friedman remembers the Band Box Theatre, which he describes as a "very small theatre with the main aisle running down the middle. After World War II, investors bought it and the property on State Street in back and created the Avon Theatre, which was far larger," he said. "You'd buy your ticket on Broughton Street, then walk through the arcade [that once was the Bandbox], cross the lane and enter the theatre."

Leon also remembers a story his mother told him about the Lucas. "I guess it was about 1926 or so, just before she married my dad, and she went to see a movie at the Lucas," he said. "As she approached the door to the theatre a tall, lanky man doffed his hat to her and held the door open so she could enter." When she turned to thank him, she saw that it was none other than Henry Ford.

Eddie Manucy and Gene "Mac" McCracken recalled the Arcadia, Folly and Bandbox being on the south side of Broughton Street between Abercorn and Drayton Streets. About the same time, the Bijou and Odeon opened on the north side of Broughton, they said. The Avon and the Weis replaced two of the smaller ones, but they can't remember which two.

Eddie and Mac remembered spending all day Saturday at either the Folly or Bandbox watching cowboy movies. The price of a ticket was ten or fifteen cents and, on some occasions, eight cents, which entitled the patron to stay all day (seeing the same movie over and over).

The Savannah Theatre was built by William Jay in about 1818 as a venue for plays, operas and silent movies, Eddie and Mac said. It was severely damaged by fires between 1945 and 1948 and rebuilt as it is now in 1950. It not only had a balcony but also was a much nicer theatre that offered better movies, including the all-popular Westerns, they added.

But long before movie watching became such a breeze, people in Savannah were going to theatres in droves. And many film buffs still recall the tiniest details of a trip to movie houses that are long gone.

Carl Milton's first memory of going to the movies in Savannah as an African American dates to spring 1968, he said. "It was after Dr. Martin Luther King's assassination and before Senator Robert Kennedy's," he said. "I had just entered my teens and my brother Charles and I would spend Saturday afternoons at the Star Theatre [on what was then West Broad Street]."

The theatre opened about 1:00 p.m., and Carl and Charles would walk the eight blocks from their home to the Star. The theatre, he added, was rapidly going downhill and smelled musty inside. But shortly after Carl and Charles paid for two seventy-five-cent tickets and entered the lobby, they forgot about the declining condition of the building. They smelled—and tasted—yummy concession stand items like popcorn, hot dogs and vanilla ice cream.

For the price of one ticket, the Milton brothers sat through two or three war movies or Westerns, such as *Day of the Evil Gun*, before walking home past 6:00 p.m.

During the next three to four years, Carl said that the audiences at Broughton Street theatres became more diverse. Westerns began to fade into the sunset and martial arts movies starring the late Bruce Lee soon hit the big screen.

Judy Brown Boswell of Clyo also grew up in Savannah and remembers going to the drive-in with her crowd. "The Weis Auto Cinema [on Montgomery Crossroad] was the happening place," she said.

Judy and some of her pals snuck into the drive-in by hiding in the trunk of a car while a couple of other buddies entered legally by riding in the front and backseats. "When we got to the ticket booth [my friends] would be banging on the backseat trying to get [those of us in the trunk] to be quiet because we'd be laughing so hard…I saw *The Exorcist* seven times and couldn't tell you what it was about until I was forty and saw it on TV."

Instead of watching the movie on the huge screen, Judy and her drive-in companions went from car to car visiting friends. The concession stand also was a popular spot. "We went to all of the drive-ins—the Montgomery, the Victory and the Highway 80—but the Weis was the best," she said.

Judy can't forget the summer when Elvis Presley died because most of the drive-ins scheduled Elvis movie marathons. "My girlfriend [nicknamed Fanny Farkle] made us go to every one of them."

HIGHWAY 17

Howdy's, Camp Juanita's and Other Colorful Spots

Denny Smith pulled his Buick into a spot on Ogeechee Road and slipped the vehicle into park. "This used to be a bar called the Windmill that actually had a working windmill," he said. He pointed to an area behind a bank building and began reminiscing about the way things used to be on Ogeechee, also known as U.S. 17 South.

For a while when he was growing up, Denny and his family lived in what was one of the tourist courts on Highway 17, which was the bustling road to Florida before anyone ever dreamed of Interstate 95. He remembers how, as a child, he and his sister were playing in the yard outside when they heard a gunshot. The owner had committed suicide over a domestic issue. It wasn't too long afterward that the tiny frame houses were demolished and another business replaced them.

The Highway 17 landscape that Denny knew as a child and teenager began disappearing once Interstate 516 sliced its way through the area. The small mom and pop tourist courts and independently owned motels became obsolete when I-95 took away the traffic from Highway 17. Tourist courts often included a handful of miniscule houses with kitchenettes and carports where travelers could check in for the night.

Denny, sixty-four, still recalls many of the businesses and characters that frequented the area that he called home. For a handful of years, his father, Elmer Smith, worked for George Cubbedge's oil company, which had offices in a concrete block building on Mills B. Lane across from the Derst Baking Company. Cubbedge had exclusive refueling rights for the train, the Orange

This vintage souvenir postcard advertised Hyde Park, one of the tourist courts on U.S. Highway 17. *Author's collection.*

Blossom Special, and Elmer and Denny often would ride together to gas up the famous train when it pulled into Savannah in the wee hours of the morning.

During a brief tour of his old stomping grounds, Denny talked about various landmarks in the area that included a Goodman's Feed and Seed. "That was Farr's Camp," he said, pointing to a vacant lot. "It started off as a tourist camp but later became rental units."

The Tremont Park neighborhood is dotted with streets named for cars, including Essex, Packard, Comet and Ford. Denny also remembers Sportsman's Park and the Patio Drive-in Theatre.

Denny can still visualize long-gone places such as Camp Juanita's, the Stanley Motel, Dot's Camp and Mom and Pop Lanier's. Howard Johnson's was the first big chain motel to replace some of the tourist camps on Highway 17, he said.

Sauers' Drugs, operated by Clarence Sauers, stood near an old oak tree at the former Sam's Club location, he said. As a teenager, Denny was a soda jerk at Sauers' and made milkshakes and such "just the way they ought to be made. It was an art to me," he said.

The Coconut Grove was a large African American nightclub that eventually burned down, and the Hyde Park Motel was owned by Johnny Hyde, who "always drove a Cadillac." Farther west on Highway 17 were "juke joints" known as Dugger's and Hatcher's, as well as the Bon Air Restaurant, he said.

Denny hung a left at Buckhalter Road and drove past the former home of Rahn's Dairy, where two silos still stand. On Garrard Avenue, he pointed out the Brown residence. "Mr. Brown owned Brown's Paint and Wallpaper near downtown Savannah," he explained.

Turning around, Denny drove east toward Savannah. Near the intersection of Ogeechee and Victory Drive is a stand of palm trees and a broken-down wooden cabin. "That was the Oasis," he said. Ironically, Highway 17 once was an oasis of sorts for tourists heading to Florida.

Another popular spot on Highway 17 was Howdy's, a restaurant with an ornate wrought-iron balcony, palm trees and flamingoes. David Oppenheim looked up the restaurant in a 1960 Savannah phone book and noticed that the Yellow Pages ad said, "Howdy Restaurant…fine food for discerning people," and was decorated with a cutout of a flamingo and the phone number "ADams 6-3465."

Like the businesses that Denny remembered, Howdy's was in its heyday when U.S. 17 was the gateway to Florida. Linda Friedman recalled going to both Howdy's and the Harvest House when she was a child in the 1950s. "I used to go to both of these places with my mom, aunt and grandmother on Sunday afternoons," she said. "I refused to sit down to eat until I had visited the birds [or the ducks at the Harvest House], and then I insisted on telling them goodbye before we left."

Dell Cone, who has lived on U.S. 17 all her life, said that Howdy's had a neon sign of a man with a top hat that he lifted up and down. Flamingoes pranced around out back and talking cockatiels entertained diners inside. During the Eisenhower administration, the cockatiels argued politics because they heard customers doing so, she said. Finally, the owner had to put a sheet over the cages to quiet the chattering birds.

FELLWOOD HOMES

Warm Memories and Lifelong Friends

Although it has been more than thirty-five years since David Coney moved out of Savannah's oldest housing project, he still has precious memories of the years he spent in the early 1960s as a youngster at Fellwood Homes. Located on west Bay Street, the project was built in 1939 and demolished in 2008 to make way for sustainable Fellwood, an environmentally friendly project.

"There was a great sense of family and community [in Fellwood]," recalled David, who called the project home from 1960 until 1972. "We knew our neighbors and would share in a time of need. Even now when I hear the word Fellwood, it takes me back to a good place and time—a time when your neighbors cared about you and your welfare."

David received a degree in electronic engineering technology from Savannah State University and writes poetry as a hobby. The title of his book of poetry, *You Are a Genius*, came from a discussion he had with SSU instructor Abigail Jordan. In the book's preface, he thanks her for "igniting a fire that still burns." Also in the book, David includes a few memories of Fellwood, among them Rita's store; Food Town and manager Abe Goodman; haircuts by Mr. Griffin; milk delivered in glass bottles left on the back porch; and the smell of crabs boiling.

David describes Fellwood as home to "many decent people." "I saw the mothers and fathers of Fellwood [going to work] making their way to Bay Street to catch the bus coming from Port Wentworth," he said. "In the evening times I would see them returning home."

David made plenty of trips to a nearby store called Ms. Rita's, which was a house that had been converted into a store.

> *It was located on the north side of West Street near Bay Street. I recall countless times going through that screen door and hearing those bells jingle...Fellwood residents and nearby neighbors frequented her store so often that Ms. Rita knew most of them by name. Customers could buy bologna, fatback bacon and ham by the slice. She also sold candy such as red hot fireballs, Mary Jane's, bubblegum cigarettes, Rock 'n Roll cookies (with pink icing), as well as pickles and pickled pig's feet.*

Growing up, David also joined in on pickup games of football on a grassy area that he and others referred to as Fellwood's "front row," which faced Bay Street. "Playing sandlot football eventually led me to Richard Hall, who was our little league football coach. He has been a leader ever since I've known him. He is now pastor of Second Arnold Baptist Church."

Ulysses "Puggy" Jackson coached the Whippers baseball team, on which David played second base. The team was established by Clarence "Cool Blue" Grant. "The year I played little league baseball, the city donated the uniforms, which said Rockets so that year [1971] we were known as the Rockets," he said. A few of David's teammates were Harry Jackson, Tim Ball, Morris Glover, Sylvester Harris, Gerald Jenkins, Tyrone Jackson, Elijah Brown, Abe Jackson, Joe Holmes, Ricky Ford, Joe Chisholm and Mack Bradham.

"We played our games at Bartow [another project] on Augusta Avenue," he added. "We played against Woodville, Bartow and Bayview and made it all the way to the playoffs at Daffin Park, where we lost."

In the summertime, David remembers the sprinklers behind the rental office. When the neighborhood children found out that the sprinklers were turned on, all of them came running, he said.

In his book, David sums up his Fellwood memories like this: "I remember shooting marbles, I remember silk and wool suits, I remember making lifelong friends."

THE PLACES WE SHOPPED

Broughton, Crossroads and So Much More

A newspaper column I wrote several years ago about shopping memories generated plenty of stories from readers who recall dozens of stores, some of which still exist and others that are long gone. Take downtown, for instance. Eleanor Faye Carter Ricks remembers a small grocery store or deli on Broughton Lane that had a donut-making machine on the sidewalk in front of the store where fresh donuts were available.

City Market, which was demolished in the 1950s, was filled with farmers' trucks and fresh vegetable bins. "There were also black women shelling butterbeans and peas and [putting them in baskets] on top of their heads," she said. Vendors also sold live chickens and fresh fish.

Broughton Street stores between Bull and Jefferson Streets included J.C. Penney's, Asher's, B. Krapf, Adler's and Sears, which later became Western Auto. Also in that area were numerous dime stores such as Kress, McCrory's and Silver's, she added. Also, Mr. Peanut walked the street and gave out free peanuts, and a roving photographer took pictures of shoppers.

Jo McLaughlin grew up in the 1940s and '50s and remembers various downtown stores, such as the Accessory Shop, Al Chaskin's, the Glendale Hat Shop, the Style Shop, Mangel's, Hogan's Department Store, Alan Barry's, Harris the Hub, Lerner's and Morris Levy's.

Paul Robinson spent time at the Hobby Shop on the corner of Liberty and Bull Streets, where he would "marvel at its huge layout of Lionel electric trains in motion over the bridge, through the town and on to the countryside." Back then, "everyone thought [the Bargain Corner at Bay and

A roving photographer on Broughton Street snapped this picture in the early 1940s.
Author's collection.

Jefferson Streets] was a giant store," he added. "But by today's standards it was a piker," he said. He also remembers paying a whopping thirty-five cents for a bacon, lettuce and tomato sandwich at Livingston's Drug Store on Broughton.

Before or after shopping, Paul might take a swim in the pool at the old YMCA at Bull and Charlton Streets. "Before entering the pool, you had to walk through a two-foot by two-foot square rubber container with low sides, filled with super chlorinated water," he said. "I'm not sure about the purpose of this procedure, but I suspect it was to make sure your feet were clean. Wow! You smelled of chlorine for a long time." The most unique aspect of the experience was having to swim in the nude, Paul said.

No doubt like many others, Harriet Hartley recalls being fascinated with a big shoe outside Dilworth's Shoe Repair on west Broughton, just a few doors from Whitaker Street. "I remember patting the toe of that shoe many times as a child when my sister walked my sister and me to my father's office at Broughton and Montgomery streets," she said. "Later, as an adult working at Savannah Electric & Power Co. [when it was on the corner of west Bay and Whitaker], I used to take shoes to Dilworth's…The Dilworths were very nice and their work was excellent."

For many years, Gail Pruitt Baxley's father, Frank Pruitt, worked at Desbouillons Jewelers on Broughton Street. Going way back, Gail's grandfather started Charles Thomas Jewelers with his brother. "After my grandfather's death, my uncle, Charles Thomas Jr., kept the store going," she said. Another of Gail's uncles, M.C. Pruitt, worked at Mewborn Jewelers and later bought it, she said. Gail worked there during the summer and at Christmas, and remembers the railroad workers "coming in to regulate their watches."

Gail also had more downtown memories, including Silva's Bookstore; Photocraft and its "when your camera clicks, think Photocraft" slogan; and Mrs. Hancock at the vocational school on Bay Street, where Gail trained to be a secretary.

Diane Duvall King shopped at Teens and Juniors on Broughton Street. A "date" meant wearing white gloves and heels to dinner and the movies downtown, she added.

She and others rode Captain Sam's first riverboat, which was called the *Visitor*. "It was a leaky old tub that frequently broke down," she said. "I remember a Sunday school [Methodist Youth Fellowship] trip when we had to be rescued by buses at Hilton Head [or Bluffton]," she said. "The light bulbs also had a way of falling overboard on night trips!"

The old YMCA was a downtown landmark. *Courtesy of Nan G. Donaldson.*

HABERSHAM SHOPPING CENTER AND BEYOND: JUNIOR'S AND WOOLWORTH'S AMONG FAVORITES

Becky Clarke Shay of Rincon grew up just down the street from the Habersham Shopping Center and snapped on her thinking cap to recall the stores in the center. On the east side of Habersham, Becky could picture Lee's Bakery and its predecessor, which was called Junior's Delicatessen. "[Junior's] sold kosher pickles out of a drum and you could buy a regular Coke for five cents and a vanilla Coke for six cents," she said.

Mary Lynn Groover Hinely of Hinesville, also from the neighborhood, had a fondness for Junior's. "Loved going in there and sitting at the soda fountain and getting a cherry, vanilla Coke, a huge kosher corned beef sandwich…Junior's was the place to hang out when you were older."

"My parents stayed on 60th Street after I married and left home," she said. "When we would come home on vacation, my mother took my kids down to [Lee's Bakery] to get donut holes," she said. "As they got older, they would walk down there and get their 'bag of holes.'"

On the west side of Habersham, in the larger portion of the center, Becky remembers Whipkey's Drugs. "When I was about eight, my grandmother, who lived with us, was frying fish and splashed hot grease on her foot," she said. Becky hopped on her bicycle and rode as fast as she could to buy salve for her grandmother's foot.

It was customary for Becky to walk to Woolworth's (in the center) with fifty cents burning a hole in her pocket.

> *I would shop that whole store looking for just the right thing. My sisters and I laugh all the time about the time we went to Woolworth's to buy gifts for both Mama and my grandmother. We didn't have a lot of money for presents and ice cream for us so we bought a lace handkerchief for* [Mama and grandmother] *to share and an ice cream sandwich for each of us. We thought it was a good plan at the time but we were teased about it for years.*

Debbie Slotin Favale, who lived around the corner on Battey Street, recalled "great stores" in the Habersham Shopping Center. "We had everything we needed right there," she said. "From the Winn Dixie on one end, to Junior's on the other end [and opposite side of the street]. We could buy kids' clothes at Punch & Judy and ladies' clothes from Laurette's. We had a Firestone, a dry cleaners, a beauty parlor and many more stores that elude my memory."

Woodford Brown remembers Junior's as being the "anchor" of the stores on the east side of Habersham. "In the early days of that little [center], the bakery was located between [what is now Hirano's and Clary's]," he said. "Star Laundry was on the corner, and sandwiched in there was the Eagle Shoe repair shop." The parking lot and the buildings housing Rite-Aid, Bay Camera and Habersham Beverage was a vacant lot, he added. "This lot had some very old oaks and a variety of tall weeds, which made a great 'park' for the neighborhood kids to spend their summers."

Irvin Levin listed several retailers and shops: Garvin's and/or Craven's Bakery, Jimmy's Barber Shop and the Eagle Shoe Repair Shop. Another reader mentioned Marlin's shop for homes, which sold everything from party supplies to kitchen items and everything in between.

Meg Braun bought back-to-school footwear at Stewart's Shoes in the Habersham Shopping Center. "We always walked (or ran) up and down the little staircase and pedaled on the roundabout ride to make sure the shoes were 'a good fit,'" she said.

"At Byrd Brothers Supermarket in the Medical Arts Shopping Center [on Waters Avenue], the aisles were named for Savannah streets (i.e, Bull, Habersham…)," she added. "That's how I would find my mom in the store. She would say 'meet me at Bull Street.'"

Meg also remembers shopping for clothes at Lad 'n Lassie on DeRenne Avenue across from the giant globe and buying ice cream at the Yum Yum Shoppe just around the corner on White Bluff Road. "The Custom Cleaners man always brought Juicy Fruit gum when he delivered the dry cleaning," she added.

Juli Jones Williams also shopped for Easter dresses and such at Lad 'n Lassie, where lifelike child mannequins stood in the display window. "I've never seen another one like [the small crying boy]," she added.

A few doors down from Lad 'n Lassie was United Five and Ten, where Juli and her sister Barbara loaded up on Barbie doll accessories as well as caps for toy guns. "Daddy bought his liquor from the Decanter, which was next to the huge Globe," Juli said. "My sister and I loved going with him because the men working there always gave us blue lollipops.

"Other nights we'd pile in the car when Daddy drove to the DeRenne Pharmacy. While he chatted with pharmacist Don Overstreet, we'd read

These members of Entre Nous sorority may have purchased their finery downtown. *Bottom row, left to right*: Helen Kline, unknown, Nancy McMillan, Ann Eitel, Ann Brown, Mignonne Cheney and Betty Bailey. *Second row*: Hallie Atchison, Nancy Lasseter, Janet Barnett, Ann Gleaton, Eleanor Ellis, Monica Ulivo, Margaret Broderick, Peggy Mulherin

comic books from a revolving rack by the front door," she said. "On the way home, Daddy was easily talked into stopping at the Globe restaurant for a milkshake," she added.

Just behind the restaurant was the DeRenne Chrysler-Plymouth dealership, Juli recalled. "Daddy owned a 1959 Chrysler Saratoga that he'd take there for servicing," she said. "Since it was one of only two Saratogas in Savannah, the car got a lot of attention each time [he brought it in]."

and Eveylyn Hartford. *Third row*: Sara Louise Shroeder, Susan Hill, Betty Sheffield, Ermine Claghorn, Anky Kraft, Bee Varnedoe (sponsor), Peggy Worrell, Lou Stanley, Ann Tew, Priscilla Woodward, Dinky Crutcher and Carol Earnest. *Courtesy of Nancy M. Manucy.*

Midtown: Mom and Pop Shops Offered a Little Bit of Everything

Martha McCarthy Wood grew up on Bee Road in the Burtondale area during the '60s and remembers Donaldson's Supermarket by the Franklin Apartments and Vermillion's Drugstore on Waters Avenue, which "we would frequent on our daily walk home from school at Blessed Sacrament."

Weiner's grocery store on East Broad Street stands out in David Lanier's mind. "Mrs. Weiner was always very elegantly dressed, and she stationed herself at the front door so she could personally greet everyone that came in," he said.

Paul Robinson also added his two cents about shopping. Getchell's was a "great hobby-type store specializing in model airplanes, ships, etc. and located on the west side of Waters, about a block north of Victory. It was a small store, but it displayed its enormous inventory from floor to ceiling. The presentation of merchandise mesmerized youngsters like myself and caused parents a lot of grief when we spent our entire allowance there in one fell swoop."

Caroline Bontempo's parents had a house charge account at Crumbley's Drugstore on Waters Avenue, which "had a wonderful soda fountain," she said. "If you purchased a gift, such as a box of candy or dusting powder, the lady at the counter wrapped it and tied it with a ribbon. Across the street from Konter's Supermarket was Fox's Variety Store, which sold men's clothing "along with just about anything else," she added.

Caroline's father bought "delicious" German sausages at Hohnerlein's Meat Market at the intersection of Waters and Wheaton Street. For other groceries, the family shopped at Konter's, Womack's and Donaldson's.

Farther south on Waters was Red Lariscy's Service Station, 49th Street Pharmacy, Kleeman's Market, This 'n' That, the Victory Soda Shop, Whipkey's Drugstore and O&W Cleaners.

CROSSROADS AND VICTORY PLAZA: BELK'S, WOOLWORTH'S, A&P AND MORE

Martha McCarthy Wood said that her mother "constantly had us up" at the Crossroads Shopping Center and Victory Plaza at Victory Drive and Skidaway Road and recalled stores such as Jefri's, which sold women's clothing.

At Crossroads, Teresa Tuten remembered Belk, Woolworth's, the A&P Grocery Store and Elliott's Drugs. Also, the Savannah Bank & Trust Company had a separate building in the parking lot. Baskin Robbins Ice Cream was on Skidaway across from the Victory Bowling Lanes. "My first job!" Teresa said. "I also remember when there was a Dairy Queen near Chelsea Apartments [because] it was the place my dad took me after I went to the dentist."

Patti Nafis Entrekin remembers when the Diana Shop ("not as cool as Lady Jane or Town and Country") was in the Crossroads Shopping Center and Adler's was across the street in the Victory Plaza.

Readers also mentioned the Colonial Store, Grant's and Teens and Juniors.

DOWNTOWN

Santa Claus, Daddy Grace and Friends

Mary Wiggins has precious memories of growing up not far from downtown Savannah. The same goes for Bobby Harn, who was raised near the old City Market. During the 1940s, Mary and her family lived on the corner of East Park Avenue and Abercorn Street, where she remembers a series of what she called "family neighborhood bars." "There was one in our backyard," she said. "It was called 'Bill's Retreat,' and as a child, I would climb up on a stool and order a Coke and peanuts. [The people who worked there] knew that Daddy would pay later."

Bobby recalls a character nicknamed Scrap Iron who hung around the market. "He would get peaches and such that were beyond sale and make wine called scrap iron," Bobby said. Once, a few blocks over—on Franklin Square—Bobby and his buddies heard "a lot of commotion" around First African Baptist Church. They watched as a limousine pulled up and a red carpet was rolled out. "I thought I heard people around us saying that it was [well-known clergyman] Daddy Grace," he said. "I think that might have been around 1944." Also during World War II, Bobby remembers hearing an explosion coming from River Street. "People were scared and rumors were going around that a German submarine had slipped up the Savannah River and blown up the electric plant," he said. The noise probably came from a blown transformer, he added.

Broughton Street, in particular, holds fond memories for Mary. "On the Friday after Thanksgiving, there was a Christmas parade for Santa Claus to ride into town and visit with children at Adler's on the corner of Bull and

This trio of children standing at Lincoln and 39th Streets probably enjoyed shopping downtown. *Author's collection.*

Broughton Streets," she said. "When we shopped at Adler's, the clerks would put the money in a little glass case and send it upstairs in a tube to the cashier. The tube was similar to what you see nowadays at a bank's drive-in window."

Like many people who grew up during the 1940s, before the advent of television, Mary enjoyed going to the movie theatres on Broughton Street. "The Bijou was our choice," she said. "On Saturday at 10:00 a.m. there was 'Amateur Hour,' then two continued shows [*Superman* and *Sky King*], then an hour of cartoons followed by two Westerns. We would get out around four and go to the theatre's soda shop, where we listened to the jukebox and drank milkshakes."

Another favorite spot was Mr. Walsh's grill on the southwest corner of Broughton and Abercorn Streets. "I remember it well because my aunt worked there during World War II," she said. "That's where she met her future husband, who was stationed at Hunter Air Force Base [as Hunter Army Airfield was known then]. They were married and moved to Buffalo, New York."

By 1949, Mary's family had moved to a place on Henry Street between Abercorn and Drayton Streets. She said,

> *After Sears-Roebuck* [at Henry and Drayton] *would close, we would skate in the parking lot until as late as our mothers would let us. We sometimes skated around Forsyth Park. The funniest thing, though, was skating through Mr. Mamalakis's filling station at Henry and Drayton. He would come out and tell us to stop, and guess what, we would come back and do it again. Later we realized that he was only concerned about our safety.*

Mary can't forget Friday night dances at Forsyth Park. "We would play records in an old army barracks–type building and dance with our favorite boyfriends," she said. "Sometimes on Saturday nights we would go to Marilyn Youmans's dance studio on 37th and Drayton Streets for ballroom dancing."

Mary also remembers the name of the movie playing when the Victory Drive-in Theatre burned. Ironically, she said, it was *The Flaming Hour.*

Mary wishes that every child could have experienced Savannah the way she did.

SOLD ON FORSYTH PARK AND UNION STATION

A Personal Note from Polly

Eugenia Spradley admits that she is intrigued by history, especially Georgia history, and the prospect of moving to Savannah in 1942 was extremely appealing to her. That particular time, however, wasn't the most ideal time to move from a "sleepy south Georgia town to this busy, vibrant seacoast city [because] our country was in the midst of World War II," she said.

After moving to Savannah, Eugenia and her husband "had to be content with a one-room apartment in a dilapidated building on the westside." After landing a couple of jobs that weren't exactly his cup of tea, Eugenia's husband began working at the Big Star grocery store at State and Lincoln Streets, which later became a Colonial Store. Soon, Uncle Sam called on Eugenia's husband to do his patriotic duty, and he bade goodbye to his wife and five-week-old son. While her husband was gone to war, Eugenia learned to appreciate downtown living.

"Forsyth Park became [my son's] playground," she said. "The magnificent Union Station around the corner from our residence was a favorite place to sit and contemplate, and observe the hustle and bustle of people on the go."

For only a dime, Eugenia and her son could see the entire city on a bus or a streetcar. "During the summer an open-air streetcar would carry [us] to Thunderbolt or Isle of Hope to see the turtles, [which was] a great adventure for a child," she said. "And whether we rode across town on a bus or walked to church at 32nd and Drayton Streets, there was no fear," she added.

Eugenia's husband returned home from the war in September 1945. "Time had allowed Savannah to grow on me," she said. "It truly felt like home…the old Candler Hospital was the welcoming place for my daughter in 1946, and

Eugenia Spradley enjoyed taking her baby son to Union Station to watch the hustle and bustle. *Author's collection.*

then, in 1948, we were blessed with another son [born at Telfair Hospital]. The 1940s were indeed a very eventful era for us—a new home, war and three wonderful children, all native-born Savannahians," she said.

EAST SAVANNAH

Avondale, Savannah Gardens and Twickenham

Jackie Ray especially remembers several mom and pop stores in east Savannah because, while growing up, he used to work at a couple of them. One was situated on the little knoll that bordered Savannah Gardens and Deptford Homes, he recalled.

"Before John Prince bought the store it was called Mitchell's," he said. "It had a dirt floor for the most part. I worked there for some time before moving on to Collin's Grocery on Capitol Street."

Savannah Gardens and Deptford Homes were part of a closely knit eastside neighborhood that also included Tattnall Homes, Moses Rogers Grove and Pine Gardens. Nearby were Twickenham and Avondale and that neighborhood's state streets—Pennsylvania, Texas, New York and the like.

Shirley Brooks Ryan grew up on Foster Street in Twickenham and remembers the Friday night dances at the Savannah Gardens Community Center because in the late '50s, her mother, Ammie Brooks, was in charge of the dances. "They had what they called a Mothers' Club back then, and having the dances was one of the things they did," she said. Various mothers would take up the admission money—"something like twenty-five cents"—while others chaperoned or worked at the concession stand.

Shirley's posse of friends lived throughout the surrounding neighborhoods, including Gordonston. She attended Pennsylvania Avenue Elementary School through the sixth grade and was bused to May Howard for the seventh grade. "We had a whole wing of nothing but seventh-grade students from [East Savannah]," she recalled.

Earl Kirkley exercises by mowing the lawn the old-fashioned way in the backyard of a friend's home in Pine Gardens. *Courtesy of Mr. and Mrs. Harrell Roberts.*

The following year, she went to Chatham Junior High and often rode the city bus downtown. "I would catch it by the fire station on Pennsylvania Avenue," she recalled. She had a bus card, which she found in a drawer several years ago. "It still had ten or twelve rides on it," she said.

After school in Avondale, Fred "Vernon" Black gravitated toward Anderson's Grocery Store on Texas Avenue. "Ten cents bought a big Pepsi and a bag of Tom's peanuts," he said. The "grasshopper" was an old school bus that was converted into a "traveling convenience store." He also remembers playing "many games of softball" on the Alabama Avenue playground, where the park lady taught him and others how to use the hula hoop.

Vernon attended Moore Avenue Elementary School with Bobby Long, Sidney Daniel and Frank McGee. (Moore Avenue later was renamed Skidaway Road and the school's name was changed to Charles Herty.) "Tough guys" would walk through the neighborhood in the afternoon, and Vernon and Henry Martin couldn't resist smarting off to them, he said. "We were so lucky that they never [beat us up]," he added. "Either Mr. Martin [Henry's dad] or Mr. Raggio would always come to our rescue."

Martheda Humphries's family lived in Tattnall Homes, and she sometimes would walk to Penn Avenue School with LaVaughn and Verlis Mitchell. "We lived there all through our school years at Chatham Junior

Savannah Gardens kindergarten class, 1959. *Courtesy of Mr. and Mrs. Harrell Roberts.*

RDENS
-1959
EXIT

High and then Commercial High," she said. After graduating, Martheda and her friends moved to other parts of the city and didn't see each other as often.

After working at the C&S Bank for nearly eight years, Martheda was married and started a family. "When our third child was twenty-two months old, he died suddenly from the results of a polio vaccine," she said. "I cannot tell you the joy I felt when my old neighborhood crowd came for the funeral. We laughed a while and cried a while, but to know they loved me this much to come be with me" meant the world to her.

GORDONSTON

Kinzie Avenue Memories Are Vivid for Longtime Savannahian

When Cilie Huff Sutton's parents moved to Savannah from Sylvania in 1915 or 1916, they decided to live in Parkside near Daffin Park. But while they were living in that neighborhood, they heard about a beautiful area known as Gordonston, named for the family of Girl Scout founder Juliette Gordon Low. By 1923, the Huffs had found a lot and built a house at 213 Kinzie Avenue in Gordonston. The neighborhood is bordered by Kinzie Lane, Goebel Avenue, Skidaway Road, Pennsylvania Avenue and Virginia Avenue.

Both the family home and the neighborhood conjure up warm memories for Cilie. She remembers streets paved with crushed oyster shells and sidewalks throughout. "The Thunderbolt streetcar line ran right in front of our house," Cilie recalled of the home she shared with her parents and three older sisters.

Gordonston was "a great place" to grow up because of tightknit families and dear friends, such as Betty Smith and Mary King Sullivan, both of whom Cilie has kept in touch with through the years. "In the evenings, families would congregate outside and the children would play or take walks," she recalled. Often, people would gather around someone's piano and "everyone would sing," she added. Cilie remembers playing circus on the Oelschig Florist property and jumping in a sawdust pile. She described a nearby silo as an "architectural treasure." She and her friends buckled on their roller skates and practically sailed along the sidewalks. A favorite skating spot was the "powder puff," a particularly smooth portion of the sidewalk.

During the Depression, Works Progress Administration (WPA) employees attempted to teach Cilie and her friends to play softball. "They made a valiant effort," Cilie said. A few years later marked the beginning of World War II and the addition of the East Savannah streetcar, which Cilie and her friends could ride to Broughton and Abercorn Streets.

Another reason that Gordonston was a "neat" neighborhood was the history, Cilie said. The land was once a farm owned by W.W. Gordon, who was Juliette's father. Brownie Park had a beautiful fountain with a figurine whose hands spurted water and iron gates forged by Juliette Gordon Low. Sadly, the fountain disappeared and gates were later moved, but Cilie remembers them well.

Cilie and her husband Bill wanted to build in Gordonston but couldn't find a lot. Instead, they built a ranch-style home "as close as we could" just across Skidaway (formerly Moore Avenue). The name of that neighborhood is Elyod Heights because it was developed by a man named Doyle, which spelled backward is Elyod, said Cilie, who continues to hold Gordonston dear to her heart. For nearly twenty-five years she took water aerobics with a group at the Oelschigs' swimming pool and enjoys being part of the Gordonston Book Club.

"I think I was invited to be a member so that [the other members] could pick my brain about the history of the neighborhood," she said, smiling.

COLLINSVILLE/LIVE OAK

Everything You Could Want in a Neighborhood

In the 1930s and '40s, Waters Avenue between 31st and 37th Streets or so was as prosperous as the shopping areas on Bull or Broughton Streets are today. "We had everything you could want in that neighborhood," said Charlie Waldrop, reciting a list that included meat and fish markets, grocery stores, an icehouse, a laundry, a hospital, two service stations and a bakery.

Charlie, who is ninety, remembers dozens of neighborhood businesses, including Crumbley's Drugstore, Gene's Sandwich Shop, Mr. Davis' Shoe Repair, the Midget Stores (five- and ten-cent), Konter's Grocery, Charlie Russo's Fish Market and the Bon Ton Bakery, which had "delicious donuts."

Eukie Groover, who ran a service station, was an "accommodating fellow" who let some of the neighborhood boys "hang out and use his lift," Charlie said. Another character was Billy Brannen, a "teetotaler" who operated the Red Rooster Tavern. "Mr. Owens cut my hair until I went into the service," he added.

Back in the day, Crumbley's customers could have their orders delivered by teenagers riding bicycles. And who were two of the more famous delivery persons? Why, none other than Savannah mayor Otis Johnson and his brother, Paul Johnson.

Charlie graduated from pharmacy school at the University of Georgia and became a pharmacist at Crumbley's. "If I needed a suit or a shirt but got hung up in the drugstore, Mr. Newton from Lesser's Men's Quality downtown would help me," he said. "He was an old-fashioned salesman who kept a notebook with his customers' sizes and measurements. He would catch the bus and drop off whatever I needed (shirt, suit) at the drugstore."

Charlie grew up in a house with his parents, uncle and two aunts at 1130 Park Avenue near Live Oak Park, which had a playground operated by the city recreation department. There was a sliding board, two kinds of swings for both the "big kids and the little kids," parallel bars, a basketball court, a volleyball court and a clay court "where we played what we called paddle ball," he said. The "park lady" was Freda Wellbrook, who handed out the equipment and ran the park with an "iron hand." "If you didn't get the balls, bats and whatnot back into the box under the sliding board, she would put it on you pretty good and tell you that you couldn't come back to the park," he said.

The park's ball diamond was Charlie's regular hangout. "It was angled toward Mrs. Browne's house on Park Avenue," he said. "Her sweet peas took a beating [when a strong hitter came up to bat]."

A water fountain in the park ran continuously, and "one of the great things to do was put your finger over the [water] and squirt your friends," he recalled.

Nearby on Duffy Street was the Episcopal Home for Girls and the Oglethorpe Sanitarium, which was operated by "the Warings, and Drs. Quattlebaum, Bedingfield, Brown and Hardeman," Charlie said.

Back then, the area was known as Collinsville, he said. Waters Avenue School, which eventually was renamed for longtime principal Romana Riley, was a neighborhood mainstay. It's also the school attended by Charlie and his wife, the former Betty Crumbley, who was a few classes behind Charlie. Charlie and Betty both remember Miss Riley as running what they described as a "tight ship." "She would ring that bell and you'd better get yourself in school," Charles said. If not, she might pull out the razor strap for a whipping, he added. Or, maybe worse, "she would call your folks" and "you'd get another [spanking] when you got home. I'm very lucky she didn't catch me."

For the benefit of her children, Miss Riley established a program called Midget Savannah at Waters Avenue School, Charlie said. It was a miniature version of Savannah's city government in that there was a mayor, a treasurer and other elected offices, he explained. Charlie's friend Glenn Zeigler ran for fire chief and Charlie and his pals thought of a campaign slogan that went something like this: "He's a big boy with big feet that he can use to stomp out fires."

The school also had a "bank" where pupils could fill out slips and deposit money, he added. "I had enough accumulated to pay the [thirty-

Betty Crumbley Waldrop is second from the right of the sign. Her future husband, Charlie Waldrop, is fifth from the right on the third row. *Courtesy of Mr. and Mrs. Charlie Waldrop.*

five-dollar] tuition for my first quarter at Armstrong [Junior College]," Charlie said.

When Charlie was thirteen, he landed a job delivering the *Savannah Evening Press* (because his aunts and uncle worked at the newspaper, he said). He rode his bicycle from the 1100 block of East Park Avenue to 32nd Street, firing newspapers onto porches.

ALWAYS A SAVANNAH CONNECTION

A Personal Note from Polly

People who have frequented YMCA exercise classes any time in the last two or three decades can't miss Pam McCarthy, a cute, enthusiastic blonde with a contagious smile.

My friendship with Pam goes way back before our daughters, who are college roommates, began middle school together. In the late 1970s, I wrote a newspaper story about exercise and included a picture of Pam working out at the YMCA. But what I didn't know until a few years ago is that Pam's grandfather, whom she called Pops, was the late Fred Garis, a local sports enthusiast who is probably best known for organizing the Tiger Athletic Club. Legions of boys who grew up from the 1930s until the 1970s played Tiger sports under the man they respectfully called Mr. Garis.

I was stunned a few years ago when Pam casually mentioned that Mr. Garis was her grandfather. Coincidentally, my late mother, Pauline Cargill Powers—who was a star athlete in her day—had told me that Mr. Garis had been partly responsible for getting her involved in sports. In the early 1930s, when Mama was fourteen or so, Mr. Garis recruited her to be on a swim team that competed locally and at the Mid-Atlantic Championships in Charlotte, North Carolina. She had played a little golf before then and swam competitively after that at Savannah High School, Armstrong Junior College and later at the University of Georgia, where she was secretary of the swim club. She also played basketball and soccer at SHS and, not surprisingly, was named Most Athletic Girl of the 1935 class.

When I shared this news with Pam, she mentioned that her mother, Nan Donaldson, had scrapbooks that had belonged to her grandfather and she would

I found this old photo of my mother's swim team in Fred Garis's scrapbook. Mama is the tenth swimmer from the left. *Courtesy of Nan G. Donaldson.*

share them with me. The huge volumes are filled with hundreds of newspaper clippings and are truly a stroll through Mr. Garis's life as well as Savannah's athletic history.

The initial Savannah mention of Mr. Garis is September 1924, when he was named physical director of the local YMCA. Later, there are scores of articles about bowling leagues, basketball, an indoor baseball league, football and track. Each story lists familiar names of days gone by: Alphine Dowell, Jack Cay, John Lytjen—at a height of six feet, nine inches, he was dubbed the "tallest basketeer in Savannah."

One of my favorite stories is a 1928 account of DeSoto Hotel lifeguard R.E. Vickery's twenty-three-mile-long swim from Tybee Island to the Bull Street landing in the Savannah River. "The steamer City of St. Louis, *outward bound for New York, reported by wireless…passing Savannah River swimmer one mile below Elba Island light station," the article said.*

While scanning the pages looking for a mention of my mother, I was surprised to see a photograph of my father, who, with his buddy, Waldo Sowell, won the boys' junior doubles tennis championship at Daffin Park. The date was June 1, 1930, when the "Guyton boys" took the title. A few pages later, I found my mother's name in a story about the 1932 Mid-Atlantic swim meet in Charlotte. She was fourteen and competed in the one-hundred-yard freestyle as a junior woman.

Once again, it just goes to show you how small the world is.

BALDWIN PARK

Floating Cars and Clergy in Underwear

The Reverend Forrest Lanier and his family moved to Savannah—and the Baldwin Park neighborhood—in 1962, when Lanier was named pastor of First Baptist Church. David is the eldest of four Lanier boys and John is the youngest. Both can tell interesting tales about life in Savannah.

David's first impression of the city? "I remember pulling into [town] about 9:00 p.m., driving down Old Louisville Road when a horrible smell invaded the car." His parents told him that it was the smell of money because it came from the paper mill.

While the Laniers were house hunting, they stayed at Dr. E.N. Gleaton's marsh-front farm off White Bluff Road. David, who is a resident of Alpharetta, said:

> *I remember two things about living there. First, the farm was served by well water, not city water, and the water had that awful sulfur smell, which made you gag every time you took a shower. Mom had to force us to take a shower every Tuesday night and Saturday night so that we wouldn't smell like we just stepped out of a cotton field when we went to church. Second, the farm was on the marsh, and Dr. Gleaton had a little rowboat that we could use. Steve* [the second-eldest Lanier son] *and I learned early on that you don't want to be caught out in the middle of the marsh when the tide is going out.*

Eventually, the Laniers bought a home at 741 East 41st Street, a half block away from Baldwin Park. John Lanier described the house as "one of the most unusual I have ever been in." It had twelve sets of French doors, including three pairs in the front that emptied into the living room, he said.

David remembers the rainy weather that summer brought. He recalled:

> *One Sunday evening in June, the family was gathered around the dining room table eating supper, and my dad looked out the window just in time to see his little Porsche floating down the street. With no excitement whatsoever in his voice, he looked at me and said, "Dave, you and Steve go outside and pull the car back up the street." Steve and I were dressed in shorts and T-shirts, so we dutifully went outside and pulled the car back up the street. From then on, we usually parked at the far end of the lot, out of harm's way.*

Both David and John, who lives in Rome, remember across-the-street neighbors Harry and Helen Kaufmann and their family, who often would host Lowcountry boils. John spent many a Friday night at the Kaufmanns' with his brother, Jim, and the Kaufmanns' son, Robert, who was nicknamed Pooh.

"Helen would always have either boiled peanuts, boiled shrimp or raw oysters as a snack," John said. "Harry would always take a 'nip' and, on occasion, let us have a sip too. Since my father was a Baptist minister and we were the only Baptists on the block, we were outnumbered."

Across the lane from the Laniers' was the Victory Drive home of the Reverend J.L. Griffin, pastor of St. Paul's Lutheran Church. His daughter, Leah Griffin Duncan, also lives in Rome and told John a funny story about the effects of a childhood scientific experiment that John conducted in the vacant lot next to the Griffins' home.

"Often Joey Becton and I would take a magnifying glass and on a sunny day try to start a fire on the ground," John explained. Leah said that a bishop visiting her family saw smoke and, wearing only his underwear and socks, ran down the stairs screaming, "We're on fire, we're on fire!"

John Lanier considers growing up in Savannah to be a treat. "I still hold fondly many dear memories of our unusual home in an unusual neighborhood and, indeed, in an unusual city," he said.

BALDWIN PARK TO ARDSLEY PARK

Vegetable Ladies and the Knot Hole Club

Nancy McMillan Manucy remembers her east 40th Street neighborhood as teeming with activity during the 1930s and '40s. "With few exceptions, there were children of all ages in every house on the block," she recalled. "The houses were smushed together with little room for expansion, which made it easy and fun to spy on neighbors at night without being detected."

Nancy and her sister Jane, who was fifteen months older, grew up in an upstairs apartment at 529 East 40th Street. "I have many beautiful memories of our life together," Nancy said. "Our imaginations proved to be an endless source of fun and amusement."

Nancy remembers "lots of nice people" living between Price and East Broad Streets. The Bealls were on one corner (Ware T. Beall and two offspring), the Allreds with six or seven children were across the street, the Fosters had two kids and the Douglases had one grown daughter, she said.

Visiting relatives was convenient for Nancy and Jane. Their paternal grandmother, whom they called Mammie, lived in the 600 block of east 40th Street with her sons, Bruce and Charles. Their maternal grandparents—the Ingmans—and their aunts, Tootie and Bertha, lived at 910 East 40th Street.

"The Kicklighters [Clyde, Grady, Gloria and Henrietta] lived across the street. The Bremers lived next door on the north side and the Farris family lived on the south side," she explained. "The Farrises had a small river home and invited us to go fishing or crabbing with the boys. I remember the crabs, a very leaky old rowboat and a fear that either the crabs would bite me or I would drown."

W.D. McMillan with his daughters, Nancy and Jane. *Courtesy of Nancy M. Manucy.*

The Leches lived on Maupas and were good family friends, she said. "They, too, went to Blessed Sacrament and would come visit frequently. There were three Leche girls—Shirley, Lorraine and Joyce."

"That, too, was a lively neighborhood filled with many children," she recalled. "I remember learning how to play card games like pinochle, bridge, spades and solitaire either with my four boy cousins who visited every summer or with Papa and Aunt Bertha."

Bertha also spent many hours reading poetry to Nancy and Jane when their parents were vacationing. "I always slept in Aunt Bertha's bedroom, which was very cold," she said. "Aunt Bertha would heat a brick to warm the bed and Jane would sleep in my grandmother's room, where I was born, because it was larger and warmer."

In those days, seeing the ice wagon was a huge treat. Children hopped on the back of the wagon for a ride and, hopefully, handfuls of freshly chipped ice, Nancy said. "The iceman would grab onto a large piece of ice with huge tongs, slinging the chunk of ice across his shoulders that were lined with a croaker sack," she explained. "He would then slowly drag his block of ice into the homes along the way, depositing his burden in each kitchen. Those twenty stairs leading to our second-story apartment must have been quite a challenge, as they lead straight up without a landing to rest on."

Various stores also offered home delivery either daily or weekly, she added. "Who could forget the icy cold, sweaty bottles of milk (cream on top—milk on the bottom)...or the delectable pints of Annette's Dairy lime sherbet?" she asked.

Going to Tybee conjures up warm memories. "Mother would take us to Mrs. Macdougall's Boarding House...the food was delicious and the place always crowded with happy beachgoers," she recalled. "Tootie always had a nice car thanks to my uncle Bob, who owned a dealership in Miami. All of us would look forward to trips to Tybee with our friends, Liz Gilbert [Grayson] and her children, Betty and Loran. We would pile in the back seat carrying shoe boxes neatly lined with waxed paper which contained delectable sandwiches; also a large thermos of lemonade and ice."

Nancy's father, the late W.D. McMillan, was sports editor for the newspaper, so the family attended many Savannah Indians baseball games. Nancy and Jane often rode to the hotel with the stars of the team, which was unforgettable. "My cousin, Rich, was a member of the knothole club for kids under twelve and [membership] cost twenty-five cents a season," she said. "This entitled members to sit in the bleachers in left field but not a seat in the grandstand."

When her father built a new house at 606 East 52nd Street, Nancy wasn't too happy about moving out of her comfortable neighborhood. She soon adjusted to being in the "woods" with no paved roads and few playmates, but that changed quickly. Nancy and Jane played paper dolls with Carolyn Gross and Betty Ann Miller and rode bikes with Mary Carter and Marilyn Sickle.

Some of the 52nd Street neighbors were the Kuhrs, the Deans and the Martin Stelljes family, who lived next door to the Dunaways. "Frances Dunaway had a home beauty parlor in her kitchen, which came in handy," Nancy said. "She was so relaxed and everyone, including the neighborhood animals, would wander in and out of her kitchen."

During the next few years, more houses began popping up between Waters and Bull Street and southward to the Columbus Drive area, Nancy said. One memory that stands out in Nancy's mind is the abundance of fresh vegetables in her old neighborhood and her new one. Vegetables were delivered by a black woman who sang about her wares blocks away, Nancy said.

> *It seemed so hard for the vegetable woman to push a very heavy, cumbersome cart all the way from the other end of town to our neighborhood singing such a cheerful tune. One of the vegetable women was named Bertha...who followed us out to 52nd with her cart* [after the move]. *She would ask for a drink*

Nancy and Jane McMillan in front of their east 52nd Street home. *Courtesy of Nancy M. Manucy.*

> *of cool water and sit on our steps for a while measuring out the fresh butter beans, green peas and okra* [real white corn already shucked] *in pint and quart tin cans that were filled to the brim. She came to us for about ten years and I sometimes wonder what ever happened to her and her children.*

The war years were surely unforgettable, Nancy said. "Our cousins all enlisted in various branches of the service and, with the exception of my favorite cousin, Robert, all survived." Nancy remembers rationing and food shortages. "Mother bought a beef tongue (all the butcher had left) and cooked it to perfection," she recalled. "It looked like what it was—my dad laughed and we all wound up in hysterics—it looked as though someone had jerked that thing right out of the cow and slapped it on our table."

During the war, the McMillans also rented rooms to folks—"some we knew and some were strangers—a few were from Hunter Field and others who were in Savannah working with the war effort. We always had interesting conversations around the dining room table, especially when the roomers were invited to dinner."

Sadly, Nancy's father died in 1947. "He was such a beautiful person," she said. "We were lucky to have him with us. No one could ever take his place, but life did go on and we grew up in the house he loved so much."

On Sundays, Nancy, Jane and their mother attended Mass at either Sacred Heart or Blessed Sacrament, which Nancy remembers when it was a "small white church on 44th Street" and her husband Eddie Manucy's grandmother, "Ma," played the organ. "She was a tiny little lady with a lighthearted personality who enjoyed life with her family. She lived to be very old and died at the Little Sisters of the Poor on 37th Street. I truly believe that she was a living saint [who was] very devoted to God and her family."

Another memorable person in Nancy's life was her uncle Allain Ingman, whom she described as being "quite a character." She said,

> *My Uncle Allain's visits were memorable and a source of great joy to my grandmother. There was not much doubt that he was her "favorite" child, as they would talk endlessly about common interests and laugh about some of his antics. I will never forget my grandmother standing in the doorway as Allain was leaving the house headed for Vermillion's on Waters. It was so natural and touching—a mother's never-ending care. She said: "Look both ways before you cross the street."*

He was seventy at the time.

ARDSLEY PARK I

Lifelong Friends Remember Fun-Filled Days from the 1960s

Growing up in Savannah, Lokey Lytjen and Beverly Davis lived one house away from each other in the 500 block of east 45th Street. They were nonstop playmates and were in and out of each other's houses a zillion times a day. In fact, they kept water bottles in each other's refrigerators. "The idea behind this was that we would not dirty up a million glasses every day—in a time when the dishwasher was your mother," Lokey recalled. "At Beverly's we had Mrs. Buttersworth syrup bottles for water bottles. In the cap of each bottle we etched our names or our initials."

For her fiftieth birthday, Beverly received a gift from the heart from Lokey, her lifelong friend, who put together a scrapbook full of memories, including the story about the Davises' water bottles. Lokey now lives in Jackson, Wyoming, but she remembers those fun-filled days of the 1960s and '70s like they were yesterday. Ditto for Beverly, who moved back to Savannah a few years ago after living away for more than two decades. Beverly cherishes the book Lokey gave her on her landmark birthday.

Chapters in the book include "50 Thoughts of Savannah," "50 Places We've Been Together," "50 Things Southern," "50 Friends and Relatives," "50 Memories of Friendship," "50 Photographs for 50 Years" and "50 More Memories of Growing Up on 45th Street." Here are a few of the memories that were listed:

Above left: Beverly Davis. *Courtesy of Lokey Lytjen.*

Above right: Lokey Lytjen. *Courtesy of Lokey Lytjen.*

- 50 thoughts: camellias; Byrd's oatmeal cookies; Miss Williams's (Williams Seafood); and spring tide…
- 50 places "we've been": Shoney's; Chip's Hamburgers; Belk at the Crossroads; and Mack's 5 & 10 Cents Store…
- 50 things Southern: "Fixin' to"; "bless your heart"; Sunday dinner with family; and freshly washed clothes hanging on a line…
- 50 friends and relatives: Linda Norma Norton; Jeff Davis; Jack Lytjen; Jim Brown Davis; and Sandy Lytjen…

Lokey's fifty memories of friendship are priceless experiences on 45th Street, in the heart of the Ardsley Park neighborhood. The water bottle memory is one of those stories. Here are a few others that Lokey recalled for Beverly:

> *When my mother was away, my father attempted to braid my long brown hair. When he was unsuccessful, he would call* [your mother] *in the morning and ask her if she would please braid my hair. I would run down to your house with my hair stuff and she would fix my hair for school.*

One evening my parents had some people from the Savannah-Chatham Board of Education over for dinner…mother had coached us earlier in the afternoon to stay close to home so that she did not have to holler for us when it was time to come home for supper. We were not to "traipse" through the house with all of the neighborhood kids behind us…we decided to play in the front yard…we divided into two teams and kicked the football back and forth in the front yard…someone kicked the football high and to the north—right into the living room windows right into the hors d'oeuvres on the coffee table…

I cannot even remember how many nights we spent together growing up.

We shared a magical, unhurried childhood on 45th Street in my beloved Savannah—a small, lazy, Southern city.

On an earlier birthday, the ever-thoughtful Lokey presented Beverly with the following poem:

Fast Friends from Forty Fifth
By Lokey Lytjen

Black braids and brown braids playing together
On tricycles then two wheelers
Fast Friends from Forty Fifth

Making bamboo spears and "parachuting" from the Boone's garage roof
Wearing cut-off blue jeans and mainsail tennis shoes
Exploring the lanes of Forty Fifth

Pausing in the kitchen to drink water
From bottles on the refrigerator door
Then racing back down Forty Fifth

Black braids and brown pixie haircut
Walking our special route to Charles Ellis School
Wearing clothes our mothers made on Forty Fifth

Kick the can, football, Barbie, army and dress-ups
Monopoly, basketball, poker, half rubber and other games
Changing with the seasons on Forty Fifth

Washing Charlotte's head and reading about Nancy Drew or the Hardy Boys
Spending the night together and eating "oven toast" or "toaster toast"
A few houses down Forty Fifth

Lying in dew-damp grass on balmy summer evenings
Hanging out on Miss Mustin's corner on chilly winter nights
Safe and sound on Forty Fifth

Lazy childhood days spent roaming the neighborhood
Ever accompanied by a cocker and a collie
Well known on Forty Fifth

Short black hair and long brown hair; long black hair and short brown hair
Now tinged with gray. Through the years
Fast friends from Forty Fifth.

ARDSLEY PARK II

Neighborhood Brawls and Ballgames

For some reason, it's the neighborhood brawls that stand out in David Dickey's memory when he recalls his youth. David, of Savannah, lived in the 500 block of east 51st Street and remembers gory details of several fights.

"There was the time that Cary 'Shoobie' Shoob got into a fight with Pat Russell's younger brother in the lot beside the old soda shop on Waters between 50th and 51st Streets," he said, adding, "Speaking of Shoobie, and with the imagined hindsight skill of a Mills Lane referee, I declare Cary the winner. Cary was as tough as his daddy, Jay, who was, along with DeDi Mathews, one of the finest boxers ever to mount the ring in our fair, beloved city!"

The soda shop is where David first learned about inflation: the shop originally sold Cokes for a nickel at the bar and packs of baseball cards for a nickel. "My daddy would give me a dime allowance for cleaning the yard or my room, and I would march straight to the soda shop to buy a Coke and a pack of cards," he said. When the price of a Coke went up to six cents, David could no longer afford to buy both. "I faced the most serious dilemma of my young life," he said. "I thought I would die. To solve the problem, I had to work twice as hard to earn twenty cents."

David also recalls a skirmish with Tommy Lynah. The fight was broken up by Tommy's brother, Jim, who was the "football hero of Richard Arnold Junior High and worthy opposing quarterback against Julian Smiley of Myers Junior High."

Soldiers in the pine cone wars included Bill Hopkins, Andy Calhoun, Tommy Lynah, Mike Martin, John Saffold, Jess Jordan, Strud Blun, Rod

Johnson, Raymond Demere and Harvey Gilbert, among others, David said. "We used trash can lids as shields against the hard green cones," David explained. "But if one of those missiles ever penetrated the fortified defenses of 'Fort Calhoun' [as the boarded treehouse in the Calhoun backyard was called], it could leave you with a black eye."

David also wonders how many windows "old Mr. Kehoe" had to replace in his garage from having been broken by foul balls off the "29 Louisville Slugger" wooden bats of the Calhoun backyard stadium. "The most wonderful aspect of that oft-repeated incident was that Mr. Kehoe always graciously replaced the window without ever complaining about it," David said. "I guess somehow the fine old southern gentleman knew that, if his boys were in the backyard playing hard ball, they wouldn't be running the streets and getting into trouble.

The Panthers circa late 1950s. *Front row, left to right, by number*: 13, unknown; 52, David Futrell; 37, Ricky Smith; 40 and 5, unknown; 20, Neil Victor; 36, Frank Durkin; and 4, Steve Becker. *Second row*: 11, Ken Powers; 41, unknown; 56, John McElven; 29, Mark Thomas; 99, Terry Dismukes; 36, Billy Mordecai; 10, unknown;

Somehow I feel he thought it was a way he could make a contribution to the cause of raising young men the proper way."

Many bags of flour borrowed from the Calhouns' kitchen were used to draw the first- and third-base lines of Calhoun field, David said. "Whether serving as a baseball diamond, a football field or the basketball court, the Calhoun field never could yield a single blade of grass. All green life was stomped out by the relentless attack of would-be Mickey Mantles and Johnny Unitases," David said.

These boys of summer talked about the news daily and announced it to their friends while portraying Walter "Concrete" and Eric "Insecticide."

When it came time for genuine, organized football, David played for the Panthers in Daffin Park because he was friends with Mark Thomas, Ricky Smith, Jim Brasfield and Bob Williams, who were also Panthers, he said.

and 19, Glenn Hewitt. *Third row*: 33, Mike Gignilliat; 93, Lee Alexander; 25, Bill Caldwell; 74, unknown; 80, Marc Weatherhorn; 22, Jim Brasfield; and 50, Chuck Palefsky. *Author's collection.*

REMEMBERING OUR BACKDOOR NEIGHBORS

A Personal Note from Polly

Henry Tenenbaum, his wife Phyllis and their daughters, Rhonda, Bobbie and Lori, were my backdoor neighbors when I was growing up on east 54th Street. I figured that the Tenenbaums owned every board game imaginable because they had dozens neatly stashed in their den closet: Clue, Sorry, Racko, you name it and they had it. And across the closet nestled on built-in shelves was a complete set of the World Book Encyclopedia. *I remember those beautiful red and blue reference books because our encyclopedia was more like a huge dictionary. It was lacking in both color pictures and a cover, which apparently had been torn off and discarded way before I was born.*

It was often early morning when I ran out our back door, navigated the narrow walkway between the Tenenbaums' and Murrays' garages and rang the bell at the Tenenbaums' side door. Once inside, I would retreat to the den or walk past the breakfast nook and head back to the bedroom shared by the three girls. If ever we had the occasion to go into Mr. and Mrs. Tenenbaum's bedroom, I found myself mesmerized by Mrs. Tenenbaum's bridal photo, which was framed and sitting on her dresser. My mother was married in a suit during World War II, and no photo of the momentous occasion existed.

When Rhonda thinks of 55th Street, she recalls the sweet aroma of honeysuckle growing in the lane or one of my older sisters teaching her how to make cinnamon toast. "Even now, the smell of honeysuckle takes me back to my childhood," said Rhonda, who now lives in Washington, D.C. "I still pull out the center [of the vine's flower] so I can taste the honey."

Polly Powers Stramm. *Author's collection.*

Rhonda remembers all the neighborhood children "gathering on the driveway between my house and the Murrays' house to play a rousing game of kickball." She also remembers "field trips" to the woods just south of 60th Street. I am a few years younger than Rhonda, but I can picture an opening in the woods and seeing one of those short, stubby black kerosene lanterns that city workers placed in the street (along with a yellow triangular wooden sign) to mark potholes or freshly paved areas.

Rhonda was born in 1948 and came home from the hospital to the cozy, brick home on 55th Street. Bobbie was born in 1952, and Lori came along in 1956. All the girls attended Charles Ellis Elementary School, where Rhonda remembers evacuation drills during the Cuban missile crisis "when [teachers] would march us down" to the train tracks. "I used to have nightmares about breaking out of the line and running home to be with my family," said Rhonda, adding that all of the neighborhood children "met in the Mathews' house and planned how we would gather in their downstairs den and place sandbags outside the window" for protection.

Looking back to her younger days, Rhonda can picture her father's business—Tenenbaum's Food Store—which was at Bolton and Cuyler Streets, an intersection that no longer exists. "Urban renewal took it over," she explained. "As I recall, the store had concrete floors and the outside was cinder block. The street was dirt for most of the years. I can still picture the different areas in the store—where the cash register was, where we packaged rice, the meat department and the butcher block."

It was a thrill for Rhonda to ride to the store with her father and be put in charge of the "cookie department," she said. One cookie from a large clear jar sold for three cents and two cost a nickel. "I kept a ledger and my father would pay me a percentage of the sales at the end of the week," she recalled.

Rhonda said that the store was opened by her grandfather, Meyer "Pap" Tenenbaum, who came to America from Europe and settled in Chicago. Someone told him about Savannah, and he moved down and opened the store "well before World War II," she said.

When the store closed to make way for a housing project, Henry Tenenbaum went into the insurance business. Tragically, he and his daughter Bobbie were killed in an automobile accident in 1966.

Several years ago, Rhonda found a few pictures of the store and commissioned artist Ken Harrington to paint a picture of it. "It is hanging in my apartment, and I love looking at it," she said.

ARDSLEY PARK III

Preacher's Kid Confesses to Washington Avenue Hooliganism

During summer nights in the 1960s, Conrad Derrick and his buddies played a game they called "Dodge the Car Lights" in the middle of Washington Avenue, one of the most beautiful streets in Savannah. "The game involved getting out into the median after dark and running up and down it while cars passed," explained Conrad, who now lives in Florence, South Carolina. "The object of the game was to jump into the clumps of azalea bushes in the median before the car lights would shine on you. If the car lights got you before you could get to the azaleas, you were 'caught' and out of the game."

Years later, when his children were young, Conrad told them about the game, which they experienced firsthand during a visit to Savannah. Conrad parked on Washington and demonstrated the game by running with his children from one end of the median to the other.

"It was quite the déjà vu experience," Conrad said. "I'm sure if anyone saw us, they probably thought this was some kind of child molester chasing two small children down the median."

Conrad was just six when his father, the Reverend Curtis Derrick, became pastor of the Evangelical Lutheran Church of the Ascension. Conrad's mother was Rebecca Derrick. As preacher's kids, Conrad and his older brothers, Carl and Curtis, spent plenty of time making mischief at the parsonage on Washington Avenue. (Christie was the Derrick boys' little sister.)

For example, years ago on a summer morning, Conrad and his brother Carl were lying in their beds. Suddenly, they heard the clip-clop of the

The Derrick family with their mother, Rebecca. *From left*: Curtis, Carl and Conrad, with Christie in front. *Courtesy of Conrad Derrick.*

Annette's Dairy horse and milk cart coming down the street. When the milkman got off the cart and headed around to the back of their house to deliver the milk, Carl went to the window and yelled, "Giddy-up," Conrad said. The horse complied and started its clip-clop down the street. "We laughed and laughed as we watched the milkman come back from around the house and run down Washington Avenue yelling, 'Whoa, whoa.'"

Other memorable experiences happened on Sundays, of all days. Conrad and his brothers usually attended the early Sunday morning service at church and rode the bus home to have a couple of hours to themselves before their parents returned from the later service.

"Frequently, we would call the Parkside Quick Shop [which offered a bicycle delivery service] to place our order for Coca-Colas, Milky Ways and the latest edition of *Playboy* magazine," Conrad said. "Of course, we only read the articles and didn't look at the pictures. The cashier at the Quick Shop would always politely ask, 'And where do you want this delivered?' My brother, in his best deep-sounding voice, would respond, 'Pastor Curtis Derrick's house, 606 Washington Avenue.'"

In a little while, the Derrick boys would see the delivery boy huffing his way down Washington Avenue with a brown paper bag in his bike basket. "I'm sure the management at the Quick Shop probably wondered why the Reverend Derrick had such a strange fetish for three Cokes, three Milky Way bars and the latest *Playboy*—on Sunday morning no less!" he said.

Another of Conrad's neighborhood memories involves Dr. Milton Mazo, who lived across the street. "He had a swimming pool in his backyard, and he had given us permission to swim in it just about anytime we wanted to cool off," Conrad said. "We spent many afternoons, especially during the steamy summer months, enjoying that pool. Sometimes when he would get home, he would sit out there and watch us with our parents. It is hard to imagine having a doctor now who would be so kind to his patients."

Conrad also remembers when he and his brothers went for checkups at Dr. Mazo's office. "We decided that we would fool him by putting tap water in the urine sample test tubes," Conrad said. "We were all waiting in the examining room after we had pulled that little stunt, when in walked Dr. Mazo with a nurse and our charts. He looked at the charts and then turned to his nurse and said, 'That'll be three shots each for falsifying urine samples.' Needless to say, we were more than willing to give him new samples."

Conrad believes that no child's life "would be complete without exploring a construction site. One of the best was when [First Presbyterian Church] began work on an addition. We had great fun playing in the big piles of dirt before they were moved around for the foundation," he said. "Of course, we would not have been allowed to be playing around a construction site when the work was going on, but in the late evenings we would ride bicycles up and down the piles of dirt and dig trenches."

Once the bricks started being laid, the boys would build forts. "This actually continued even after the construction was complete, and for some time after the church moved into the new building, we would sneak down into the crawl space to our secret hiding place," Conrad said. The boys kept a collection of comic books and reading candles underneath the building. One day, however, the pastor—the Reverend J. Walton Stewart—heard the boys and had a surprise for them.

"When we attempted to crawl back out, we found that he had put a lock on the crawl space door," Conrad said. "We had to call out to get him to come let us out. He was not amused, and he promptly took us home and had a little pastor-to-pastor chat with our dad." No doubt, after that, the preacher's kids stayed inside for a few days.

ARDSLEY PARK IV

Playing Sports and Delivering Newspapers

It's no surprise that sports played a pivotal role in Claude Felton's life when he was growing up in Ardsley Park. For several years, Claude has been associate athletic director at the University of Georgia.

Back in the day, Claude and his family lived on Washington Avenue between Bull and Abercorn Streets in a house built by his paternal grandparents. Nearby parks were ideal for playing baseball, football and "drive-back," which was akin to football, Claude said. A popular field was Lattimore Park, which was just across from the home of Frank Maddox, Claude's best friend.

"There were a good number of boys growing up in that neighborhood several years older than me and some of my friends," he said. "We'd meet in the park after school or on Saturdays and hope that some of us younger boys would get picked for one of the football or baseball teams by the 'big guys' like Ned Gay, Richard Cutts, Ty Chan, Shelton Sanford and Bobby Riley."

Claude admits that he and Frank were overmatched physically most of the time, but being picked, usually as the last ones of the daily "draft," was a big deal. "We'd play hard and do our best," he explained. "We looked forward to one day being the 'big guys.' And one day, we were."

Daffin Park also was a favorite spot for Claude, who played baseball and tennis. "I learned to play baseball at Daffin as a member of the Panthers, organized by Tom Moore and Luke Sims," he said. "They were great teachers and coaches. Getting to Pony League age and playing on the Savannah Garden Rebels team in Ambuc Stadium was a thrill."

In 1945, Claude Felton's grandfather, Claude E. Felton Sr., and Claude's aunt, Rebecca Felton Meyer, struck a dramatic pose in their Washington Avenue garden. *Courtesy of Claude Felton.*

The 1962 Savannah Garden Rebels. *Front row, left to right*: Jimmy Kelleher, Bobby Coffee, Billy Cook, Abby Slotin, Irvin Levine and Claude Felton. *Middle row*: Lynn Smith, Jeff Bolch, Durrell Hall, Louis Hoegsted and Peter Schmidt. *Back row*: Bill Odum (manager), Ricky Hargrove, Danny Sisterin, Larry Bullis, Joe Harwell, Dicky Mopper and an unidentified assistant coach. *Courtesy of Claude Felton.*

Claude was mostly a backup his first year on a "great" team coached by Bill Odum. One player—Larry Bullis—hit a ball that went over the center field wall, across Victory Drive and into the Triple X, he recalled. "I was there and still don't know if that ball went that far or the distance has lengthened with the retelling of the story," he said.

Claude also learned to play tennis at Daffin. "I was pretty good at a lot of sports but not great at any," he explained. "But tennis is probably the one I had the most long-term success and Daffin Park was my 'home court.'"

Claude loved watching veterans like Dr. John Poindexter and Bill Miller play marathon matches on the "rubico" courts—clay, as they are also called. I remember seeing Bee Gordon play on those courts in his later years. Claude also played tennis with Ed Winn, Jim Nerrin, Will Weeks, Greg Tuttle, Dicky Mopper and Mike Kelly, who has the "best forehand in Savannah."

Claude, Ed and Dicky were members of the Savannah High Tennis Team (along with Ed Winn and Dicky Mopper) that won the 1966 Region Championship. "Howard Smith, the fine basketball coach at SHS, was also the tennis coach," Claude said. "Some of us knew more about playing the game than he did (as he will readily admit), but he was great at organizing and motivating."

When it came to basketball, Claude and most everyone else walked or rode to Hull Park between 54th and 56th Streets. "Some really good players grew up playing on those courts. I got to play with a lot of them and it was great fun," Claude said. "Years later, as a freshman at Armstrong State, I was fortunate to get a spot on the basketball team, thanks probably to the 'generosity' of head coach Larry Tapp. There were some mighty fine athletes on that team, like Tommy and Bobby Cannon, John Tatum, Jeff Aycock, Danny Sims and others."

Claude's first job was delivering the *Savannah Evening Press* by bicycle in the Ardsley Park area. "After school every day, I'd go to the corner of Bull and 54th Streets, where my papers were dropped off in a big bundle," he recalled. "There I'd roll the papers and pack them in a special canvas bag that fit over the handlebars of the bike."

Claude also has "fond memories" of being a student at Charles Ellis School. "I still remember every one of my teachers from grades one through six: Mrs. Morgan, Mrs. Adams, Mrs. Exley, Mrs. Hardy, Mrs. Paulson and Mrs. Price," he said. "The principal, Horace Flanders, was a strict disciplinarian and a great educator."

Claude recalls playing dodgeball on the playground and softball in a nearby park, getting braces while a student and one important day. "On March 22, 1956, while going through the lunch line in third grade, the lunchroom supervisor, Evelyn Miles (also a close friend of my family who actually introduced my parents to each other), called me into the kitchen and told me my mother had given birth that morning to a baby brother, Forrest—later to become known as 'Beaver,'" he said.

NATHANIEL GREENE VILLAS

Sitting on the Stoops Enjoying Family

Mickey Wallace is certain that there were cold days in the late 1940s when her family was living in Nathaniel Greene Villas, but all she can remember are fun-filled summer days and nights. Nathaniel Greene was a community of working-class families ensconced in an area stretching from Bull to Habersham Streets and bordered by 56th and 58th Streets, Mickey said.

"There were no sidewalks in our neighborhood, just teeny front yards with nice bushes fronting the entrances of concrete steps and little stoops," she explained. "The narrow asphalt streets were slanting downward and before reaching Jefferson turned into swell hills for bike coasting and skating."

The wooden units were laid out in blocks of four two-story duplexes anchored by one-story bungalows at both ends, she recalled. And, although the front yards were small, "oh my, the backyards were actual meadows." The backs of the 56th Street houses looked out onto the backs of the 57th Street homes, and the "immense green spaces between the blocks" were perfect playing fields, she said.

"At the top of 56th Street on Bull across from the church—where we cowered one year as a hurricane threatened—was Reed's Market, a magical place with comic books and junk food," she said. "I'm sure other stuff was stocked, but certainly nothing that interested us kids. Best of all," she added, "in the empty lot next to the market were benches with their backs to Bull. The benches faced a blank wall where movies were shown. It was a fine time when those images filled that 'non-screen' and we all filled up with junk food from the store."

Mickey remembers a nearby service station with candy and a drugstore that sold cherry Cokes at the soda fountain. "One block down from Bull was Lincoln, a short stretch of street where the community center stood," she said. "Dances were held there and surely other activities which have left my mind," she said. "I did get my first kiss there when we played Spin the Bottle." Later, the building was moved to Daffin Park, where it is still used as a recreation center.

Early evenings were "play-in-the-front" times while waiting for supper. Afterward was radio featuring Amos 'n Andy, Jack Benny, Edgar Bergen and Charlie McCarthy, Grand Central Station and mystery stories with "creaking doors and screams in the night," she said. "You could hear it all through open windows (no air conditioning then)," she said. "The sounds shaded and warmed the comforting feelings of home and neighborhood. And at bedtime, when all the kids were called home for bath and nighty-night, I chose to climb out the window onto the roof of the next-door bungalow, shimmy down a tree, hop on my bike and fly away into the night, I know not where."

Mickey regrets that children today "don't have that wonderful sense of neighborhood, the outdoors and playing simple games with other kids, of walking and running safe and shady streets," she said. "I wouldn't trade those days for anything," she insisted.

UNFORGETTABLE RESTAURANTS

The Triple X and Johnny Harris, to Name a Couple

Ask most anyone who grew up in Savannah to reminisce about local restaurants and you're guaranteed to hear an earful about the eating establishments they frequented. Paul Robinson, for example, can't forget the Triple X Drive-In, or "the X," as it was nicknamed—the former Victory Drive landmark where everyone would spend time "schmoozing with everyone in neighboring cars."

Likewise for Dotti Overstreet, who described the X as the "the place to see and be seen." If she were lucky, Dotti would tag along with her older sister and order a Juicy Pig. "Why were those Juicy Pigs so good?" she asked. "I still haven't found a barbecue sandwich that rivals those old memories."

When Angela Hebert Straight visited her friend Anne Halligan in Gordonston, the two would walk from Anne's house to the X. "What a wonderful, happy time it was to walk carefree with friends."

Eleanor Shell Kiel remembers counting her pennies for a fifteen-cent hot dog at the Triple X. "It had a truly special taste because [it only had] sauerkraut and mustard on it and the bun was steamed," she said. "I haven't had one as good since the fifties."

At the X, boys would visit from car to car, but it wasn't cool for the girls to do the same, she added. "I'm sure many readers will remember the phrase, 'Let's go to the cemetery.'"

The root beer floats at the X were a favorite of Gail Pruitt Baxley.

After cruising around town or going to Tybee on Sunday afternoons, Eleanor Faye Carter Ricks and her friend Rochelle McGrath Brown would

The Sapphire Room at the Hotel DeSoto was a popular spot for many couples. *Courtesy of Mary Frances B. Hendrix.*

stop by the X or Our House (farther east on Victory Drive). Eleanor also remembers Cleve Ellis's restaurant farther east on Victory Drive across from Our House. Paul Robinson specifically remembers a "scrumptious" Our House dessert called the Black Beauty.

Allean Kenney of Macon enjoyed Remler's Corner and Johnny Harris's. "Who could forget the dark blue ceiling with stars and the wonderful dance floor and live music?" she asked. Allean also remembers how the boys from Benedictine Military School frequented Jerry George's on Bull Street.

Martha McCarthy Wood spent time at Shoney's on Victory Drive (next to Johnny Harris's), where the Big Boy statue stood out front. "They had curb service, and on the weekends, teenagers with new driver's licenses would drive back [to the drive-in area] and make the loop with loud playing radios."

The tiny Krystal on Drayton Street at Broughton Lane was another unforgettable spot. "In the winter, it was so warm and the windows would be all steamed up," Gail added. "How I would love to experience that again."

Sam Gaspin's family owned the Custard Bar, a drive-in restaurant that was on Bull Street and Maupas Avenue near Paul's Soda Shoppe. The popular spot was open twenty-four hours a day, he said.

My own memory was jogged when Diane Duvall King mentioned a Thunderbolt restaurant called Neptunalia. I remember breathing in the

NuGrape

One member of this bowling league was sponsored by Remler's Club Royale. *Courtesy of Nan G. Donaldson.*

scrumptious aroma of seafood as the family station wagon bounced along Victory Drive past the restaurant. "They had the best house dressing," Diane recalled, adding that the Steak House, which stood near the Casey Canal, had great jazz and scrumptious cheese spread.

On Sundays after church in the 1960s, Randy Brannen's father took the family to the Krystal on the corner of Victory Drive and Bee Road. "After Kelly's [hamburgers] was built, he took us there for a while," Randy recalled. "We went to the Dairy Queen/Brazier around the corner on Skidaway a few times. We also went to the Mai-Wai Restaurant on the southwest corner of Skidaway and Victory. We respectfully kept our Sunday go-to-meeting clothes on to go in there as it was the 'nicest' restaurant in the area," he said. "In later years, Dad started taking us to Carey Hilliards farther down Skidaway after church…I always ordered the barbecue plate. I don't believe we ever went to restaurants except on Sundays. Mom was a stay-at-home mom, and Sunday was her day of rest."

SOUTH OF COLUMBUS DRIVE (SOCO) I

Christmas Tree Forts and Sycamore Ball Battles

Rafe Semmes grew up on the corner of Reynolds and 59th Streets, the latter of which later was renamed Columbus Drive. He remembers the lane as a "special place, indeed…and a great place to play. The lane behind our house was where I first learned, at six, to ride a bike—a fire engine red twenty-inch beauty I rode until I turned twenty, and then received a burgundy and silver twenty-six-inch Murray for Christmas," he recalled. "I rode those bikes all over town during those years. It was the same sense of freedom one has with one's first car."

Rafe and his brothers would ride to nearby Jacob G. Smith Elementary School and tear around the sidewalks and go for refreshments in the Habersham Shopping Center. "You could also find blackberries along the fence behind Joe Jurgensen's house on 60th Street, across from Jacob G.," he added. "We picked buckets of them over the years. We rode bikes to Daffin Park, to the public library [on Bull and 36th Streets], even to the old bowling alley a block south of DeRenne Avenue on [White Bluff Road]. We rode them everywhere!"

Hull Park, between east 54th and 56th Streets, was another popular destination. "We usually rode down the lanes to get there, instead of the streets," he recalled. "Looking at the backs of the houses on the way always seemed to be more interesting, because you usually never saw them, otherwise. Sometimes we'd go by a house with a big dog in the backyard, and it would come running up to the fence, barking like crazy as we went by. We always pedaled as fast as we could then, just in case it somehow jumped the fence and came after us. (They never did, but you never knew.) A big dog, or a loud one, was a fearsome thing to an eight-year-old boy."

The day finally came for high school, and riding bikes and playing in the lanes no longer appealed to Rafe and his friends. "I remember distinctly that at some point, being seen riding a bike seemed very childish, so I stopped for a while, and started walking everywhere instead. (This was before kids having cars became so common. We might borrow the family car for a weekend date, in our junior or senior years, but no one to speak of had their own car back then.)"

When Rafe was much younger, he spent Saturday mornings doing chores before he was allowed to play.

> *My next-door neighbor, Oscar Brannen, and I would get on our bikes and ride over to the Savannah Youth Museum (as it was called in those days), two blocks east (near 60th and Paulsen Streets). We spent many Saturday mornings absorbed in the Indian display, watching the snakes crawl around in their cages or being mesmerized by the multicolored streaks of light in the rock display when the black light was turned on and the black curtain to the rock room was pulled shut.*

Afterward, Rafe and Oscar might wander across the street to a patch of woods where Calvary Church and school are now and hunt for lizards down by the little creek that ran through it. The daring duo hoped to "spot a real, live, honest-to-God wild snake or a possum," he said. "I remember being so disappointed when those woods were cleared to make room for that church."

If they had a little money, the boys would ride to the Putt-Putt on Bee Road and play all morning for a dollar. If they had enough left over, they'd go next door to the original Krystal on the corner and get a round waffle or a couple of miniburgers before going home. "You could do a lot with a dollar back then," he explained.

Often Rafe and Oscar would play catch in the lane behind their houses or go up and down it searching for treasures in the discards people left next to their trash cans. Christmas week, he said, always was the best time for treasure hunting in the lane.

> *Who knew what we might find after Christmas? We also had great fun every year, lugging home people's discarded Christmas trees and building two circular forts in our adjacent yards. My brothers and I would get in one,*

and Oscar and Billy Morrison from two doors west would get in another. We'd throw pine cones at each other across the fence and pretend we were defending our forts from Indians and such. Ultimately, our dads would make us return the dried-out hulks to the lane behind our houses for trash pickup. We always hated to see that day come. But a week was about as long as those things would last, before they became too dried out, the needles fell off (providing no cover) and they became fire hazards.

One year, Rafe and Oscar discovered that they could take the brown husks of sycamore balls, roll them in mud, let them dry and—almost magically—the balls would be transformed into missiles to throw at each other across the fence separating their yards. "The best thing about that was when one of those missiles hit anything solid, the mud would fall off, and then it couldn't be thrown back across the fence at the original thrower because it would be too light. We felt so smart at having discovered that trick."

Garages also were enchanting places because many of them were filled with workshops or old tools.

Mr. Hart had one such workshop in his garage, directly behind our house. He would be in there for hours, on weekends, working on projects of various kinds. Dick and his wife Charlotte have both gone on to their rewards...but I always remember the smell of wood shavings on its floor when I go by and see it, and Mr. Hart kindly taking time to show us what each of his tools would do, when we asked him about something.

In Rafe's eyes, Savannah was a much different place back then. "We never worried about anyone breaking in our houses or our cars and none of us could get very far without being under the watchful eye of someone's mother," he explained. "If any of us got out of line, a window would fly up, someone's mom would call out to us to stop whatever it was we were doing that we shouldn't and before we could run home to hide, our moms would be at the door with stern looks on their faces."

LANES WERE ENCHANTING, MAGICAL PLACES

A Personal Note from Polly

These days, my house doesn't back up to a lane, but while growing up on east 54th Street, I lived on a lane and always thought there was something magical about it. Our house was set way back on the lot and bordered the lane. Make no mistake about it, it was a lane—certainly not an alley, which is a word some people use interchangeably with lane. The word alley, however, conjures up a mental picture of a narrow, dark corridor with mean tomcats hissing and prowling about. In my day, it was quite the contrary.

Lanes were places where wildflowers grew and shrubs sprang up because people took pride in tending to the strip of property behind their homes, even though it wasn't rightly theirs. Fences of all kinds stretched up and down our lane from Paulsen to Harmon Streets. One day, I was among a group of kids that walked the fences all the way to Paulsen—a distance of about six or seven houses. It was an adventure one of us dreamed up to occupy our time. It was unheard of to bother one of our respective mothers with a preposterous question like, "What can we do?" Instead, we used our imaginations.

We started our trek by hoisting ourselves up on the chain-link fence that separated my house from our neighbors. Then, we tightroped from tree to tree grabbing what we could—the carport gutters, the side of the house and a large cherry laurel tree that hugged the lane. Our journey was a bit easier when we turned the corner into the wilds of the lane and encountered a sturdy brick fence. Next, we ran smack dab into a garage. We couldn't go under it or around it, so we went over it. Someone made sure the coast was clear, and we gave one another boosts to make our way up to the shiny tin roof. We crab-walked a bit and then slowly slid on our bottoms to the connecting fence.

Another garage with a tin roof was the end of the line; on the other side was a tight clump of bamboo. Beyond that? A vacant lot. Scanning the area for any adults who might yell at us, we again quickly made our way to the roof. What came next was pure fun. We slid down the roof into the bamboo, laughing and squealing all the way. It's a wonder any or all of us weren't impaled by the bamboo or had our eyes poked out.

Just the other day, I was driving south along Reynolds Street south of Columbus Drive when I noticed a sign that said "Enchanted Lane." I found myself remembering those days walking the fence and thinking, "Yep, that's right. Lanes were enchanting places."

SOCO II

Debbie Slotin Favale Thinks of Family and "Ev," Her Other Mother

Although Debbie Slotin Favale has lived in New Jersey for years, she still remembers her hometown and her old neighborhood with great affection. Recently, she glanced through her 1972 Savannah High School annual and read some of her classmates' handwritten messages that seemed to take on a running theme: "Don't worry Debbie, you'll make it out of Savannah!"

Debbie did leave Savannah, but at the reflective age of fifty-five, she says she can't remember why she was so anxious to go. "Perhaps I felt I must, as a rite of passage," she mused. When she recalls the years that she lived here—from the mid-1950s to the mid-1970s—she feels "special and privileged to have been born, raised and educated in this grand historical city."

Debbie looks back with "so many nostalgic memories" that she finds herself yearning to turn the clock back to when she grew up on Battey Street, a few blocks south of Columbus Drive. Just before she was born in 1954, her family moved from a Victory Drive apartment to a new house in the "suburbs" on Battey Street, between Lamara Drive (62nd Street) and 63rd Street, she said. But shortly after the Slotins moved, they were divorced, and "the landscape" of the family changed, Debbie said. The change, however, brought the addition of Evelyn Holmes, who was Debbie's "black mom" and her "favorite person in the whole world."

Not only was she Debbie's "nursie," but Evelyn also ran the household. After the divorce, Debbie's mother, Sylvia, decided that she needed to work and chose real estate. As a result, Evelyn became the "stay-at-home mom" for the Slotin kids—Judi, Marc and Debbie.

Debbie was proud of her mother's business acumen and adored her older sister and brother, but "Ev," as she called Evelyn, was a major player in her life. "Ev kept my world orderly and doted on me," Debbie said.

Playing outside was "big in our world," Debbie continued. Her best friend, Tina Kolgaklis, who was a year younger, was her backdoor neighbor

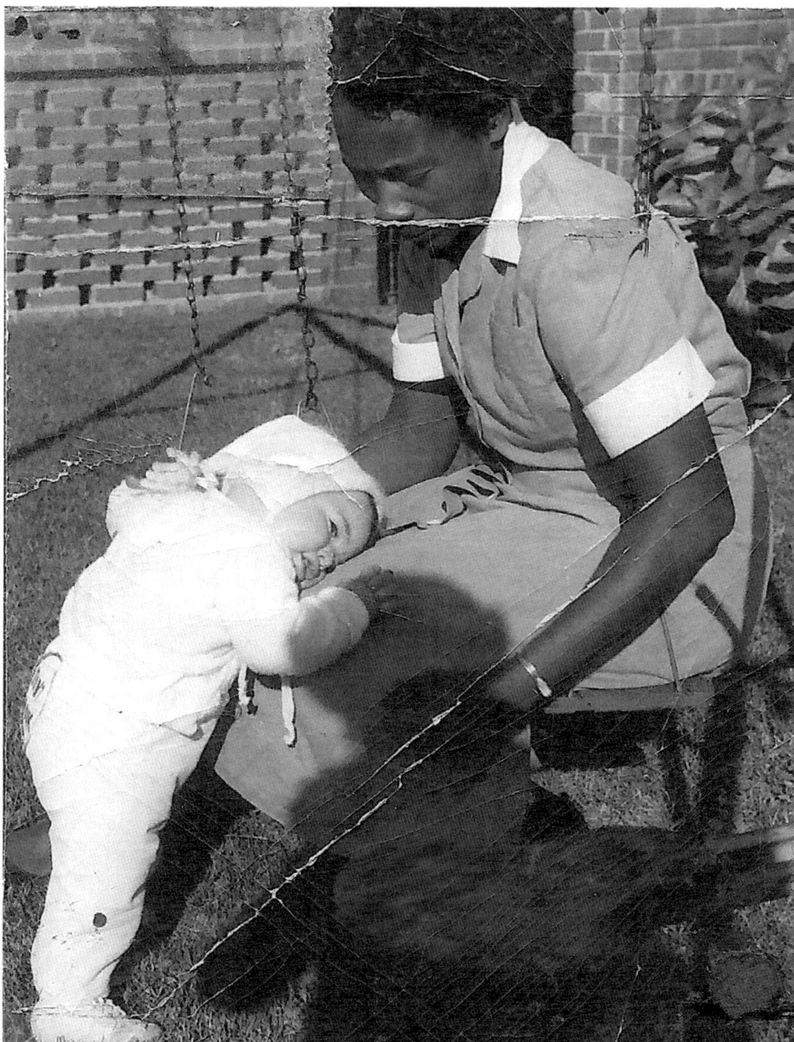

Debbie Slotin Favale referred to Evelyn Holmes as her "black mom." *Courtesy of Debbie S. Favale.*

and lived across the lane. Tina's brother, Teddy, and Debbie's brother, Marc, were close in age and were best friends. "We were always so happy when our brothers would actually play outside with us," Debbie said. "Many nights we would play outside until dark. Only then would you hear all the neighborhood parents calling that it was time to come inside."

Debbie attended Jacob G. Smith Elementary School, which was on the corner of her street. "Before I was old enough to go to school, I used to watch out my front windows and long to be old enough to start school," she said. "When I finally was able to go, [Marc] walked me to the first-grade line. I loved school immediately."

Debbie was a "talker," and her mother often took calls from the principal, who had to break the news to her that, once again, her youngest child was standing in the corner, Debbie said.

Debbie loved playing on the swings and such at school, but "sometimes on this wonderful playground the kids would taunt me" for being chubby, she said. "Most learned very quickly not to tease me because Ev told them there would be consequences to picking on me. She was my great protector."

Debbie realized all too soon that society was racially segregated. "I hated this, and even at a young age spoke out against these practices, and could be monstrous to those who promoted actions of racism…After all, I had a black mom."

Evelyn, though, had a keen sense of humor. Once, she and her friend played a joke on Debbie that Debbie says she won't ever forget. "When I was about six or seven, Ev told me I should put on a pretty outfit," Debbie said. "She said she was going to take me to meet a real celebrity. I remember putting on my patent leather shoes. We walked a few blocks to a corner house and entered through the kitchen. Sitting there on a stool was a woman who was the spitting image of Aunt Jemima. I was awestruck. I was chubby, so Aunt Jemima was like a heroine to me. She made the best waffle mixes," Debbie said. Evelyn and her friend died laughing, and even then, Debbie wouldn't let go of the idea that the woman was Aunt Jemima. "Sadly, well into my teens, I still believed that she was the real deal."

Debbie adored sitting on the screened-in back porch. "It never mattered to me if the afternoons were hot or the evenings sultry because I loved sitting on the back porch and smelling the blooms on the enormous magnolia tree in our backyard."

A few years ago, she rode by and was shocked to see how different her childhood house looked. She thought about it for a moment before she realized that when her family lived there, the trees and bushes were new and

The Slotin children, Judi, Marc and Debbie. *Courtesy of Debbie S. Favale.*

small. Although her late mother sold the house in the mid-1970s, Debbie considers 4607 Battey Street "home."

"It was built by my parents and I loved it," she explained. "I still have [recurring] dreams where the setting is that house. I will always carry around so many memories that I access by some smells, music I hear, old photos and those dreams. These precious memories, as much as I want to share them, can never really be shared. It's a feeling—a spirit that lives on in my heart and my soul, and it has shaped who I am today."

PARKSIDE

Memories of Daffin Park and Folks Helping One Another

Retired State Court Judge David Elmore grew up in the neighborhood known as Parkside, which borders Daffin Park, the midtown oasis where in the 1920s the grass was cut by horse-drawn mowing machines.

"The soldiers from Fort Screven would camp overnight in Daffin Park on their way to Fort Benning," Elmore recalled. "They would take out their horses, their latrines, tents and kitchens. The next morning, they would be gone before first light."

One of Judge Elmore's most vivid memories of Daffin is the old pool,

> *where kids could swim for five cents, but had to take a cold shower first. When you could pass the proper test, you received a swimmer's button, which allowed you to swim in the deep side, which was about ten to twelve feet deep. The two sides were separated by a boardwalk. There was a tower for those who liked to high dive and do acrobatics. And there were metal floats way out to practice swimming back and forth. Canoes and rowboats were for rent for those who liked to be out in the lake.*

Hot dogs, tobacco and other sundries were available on the pavilion, which had a roller-skating rink on the second floor. "The covered pavilion extended around the shallow side of the pool, as a place for spectators to view the scene from benches," he said. "We kids always walked from our houses in Parkside to the pool, where in the summer we spent the entire

This house is at 1220 East 50th Street in Parkside. *Author's collection.*

day swimming and playing, except for walking home at lunch time for perhaps a banana sandwich with lots of peanut butter and mayonnaise and a glass of milk."

Judge Elmore also recalls watching the Georgia Hussars, whose armory was located at the southwest corner of Bee Road and 47th Street (now Washington Avenue). "The building had two stories, the lower of which were stables for the horses, and the upper a meeting room (and at times a ballroom) for the troops and their dates. The corral was out back where the horses were turned out during the day. Captain A. Lester Henderson was in command of the troops, then designated as Troop A, with Troop B being stationed in Hinesville."

Every Monday about 7:00 p.m., Troop A would come riding west on 47th Street to the drill grounds at 47th and Live Oak Streets, where lights had been installed, he said. The guardsmen would practice riding at full gallop and try to thrust a saber through a target. Family groups would assemble each Monday night to watch the action.

"Part of Daffin Park had a shallow wading pool, no longer in use now," he continued. "But the concrete bottom made a good place to roller skate. The sidewalk on 47th Street on the Daffin side was double paved so that it made a route to skate from our neighborhood to the little pool, as we called it. Playing tag or skating in the little pool was great fun. During cooler weather, we played lots of touch football, capture the flag and other games in Daffin Park."

Because there was no drainage in the park then, parts would lie under standing water for days. "The frogs had a ball and could be heard for a great distance," Judge Elmore said. "Their croaking at night made the perfect sleeping lullaby."

The Reverend John Ashley added a poignant memory about growing up in the Parkside neighborhood. At the start of the Depression, the banks closed and his father couldn't cash his paycheck. Al Orsini (of Orsini's Market) took money out of his cash register to lend to John's father. "When my father could cash his check, he paid him back in full," he said. "People helped each other."

PARKSIDE II

A Boy's Bus Ride to Adventure

The following essay about the Parkside neighborhood was written by James Brasfield, who teaches at Pennsylvania State University. He is a graduate of Savannah High School and Armstrong Atlantic State University. Twice a Senior Fulbright Fellow, he earned a master's of fine arts degree from Columbia University. A collection of his poems, Ledger of Crossroads, *is being published by Louisiana State University Press. He has won fellowships for poetry from the National Endowment for the Arts and the Pennsylvania Council on the Arts, and also the PEN Award for Poetry in Translation, for* The Selected Poems of Oleh Lysheha *(Harvard University Press).*

It is a Saturday morning and I am waiting alone for the 20 Parkside bus. I am standing at the northwest corner of East 50th and Ash Streets, beside an orange rectangle painted on a creosote pole, on which reads, in block letters, BUS STOP. I am on my way downtown, from my neighborhood of compact bungalows and live oaks to the East Broughton triangle of dream houses: the Weis, the Lucas and the Avon Theatres. The Avon, home to second-run movies, is next to Woolworth's at Broughton and Abercorn, where the 20 Parkside has a stop. I am about to flee with Moses, or ride with the Duke, or rebel with *Spartacus*, or die with *300 Spartans*, journey *20,000 Leagues Under the Sea* or follow *The Journey to the Center of the Earth*...adventures for the price of a child's ticket and two bus tokens.

For days afterward, I will be what I have seen. Alone in my backyard, I might step from a phalanx of Spartans, a six-shooter at my hip and, as Tom Thumb, let fly a sycamore ball from my kerchief and nail Goliath, who is stepping from Federal troops gathered for assault on Fort Pulaski. History, then, is still for me the slow chaos of a cosmos forming before I understand clearly that the sun is a star, our bare bulb in the universe, our projector of light through our bijou of darkness.

I board the bus and the loop of the 20 Parkside will shuttle me through Savannah's rings of time and place. Looping north from the Parkside "suburbs" of the 1940s, crossing Victory Drive onto Drayton, I will journey back through centuries of architecture, back to Oglethorpe's squares of 1733, his vision for those in debt, and the bus will turn onto East Broughton, Main Street Savannah.

My fellow passengers are mostly neighborhood residents or African American women who work for the white families of Parkside. The women, often dressed in white uniforms, are known as "cooks." Other than domestic work, there are

Jim Brasfield (number 22) played football for the Panthers in nearby Daffin Park. His teammates were, *by number, front row, left to right*: 47, unknown; 75, Bobby Freeman; 36, Billy Mordecai; 29, Ken Powers; 18, unknown; 36, Frank Durkin; 33, Mike Gignilliat; 6, 10 and

too few job opportunities for black women, and for my mother, employing a maid is not an aristocratic notion: there are no day-care centers. The evolution of history will terminate the 20 Parkside. Until then, Sadie Gadsen, our cook, will arrive on Monday and assume again her job as my surrogate mother.

My mother, a widow, will work most of her life as an accounting clerk. Each weekday, Sadie walked me to kindergarten and was waiting for me there when kindergarten was over. She waits for me each day when I return from Charles Ellis Elementary. After I graduate to junior high, Sadie will leave Savannah for New York and better wages.

No one questioned the towheaded boy of eight or nine sitting alone at a window on the long bench seat at the back of the 20 Parkside. I had the vista of the bus and its route in front of me and the passing scenery of the city. It

5, unknown; and 24, Bobby Anderson. *Top row*: 41, unknown; 4, Steve Becker; 96, Frank Emile; 25, Bill Caldwell; 14, Ken Rudd; 56, John McElven; 29, Mark Thomas; and 82, Tommy Myers. *Author's collection.*

makes no difference to me the race of the person I am sitting beside. When where one sits on a bus became an issue in Savannah, a white adult told me that I should never sit "back there."

I force myself to find the compromise seat on the vague border between the front and the back of the bus and am reconciling, consciously or not, John Wayne (cowboy or trooper, killing "Indians") with Kirk Douglas (the slave Spartacus fighting injustice and galvanizing change—Spartacus who was certainly no "pointy-headed intellectual," or, in later common parlance, an "elitist"). And though I share a birthday with Robert E. Lee, how I would have been thrown into further moral turmoil had I, traveling in a time machine, seen Matthew Broderick as Colonel Robert Gould Shaw in *Glory*, a man of action who relished Emerson and Hawthorne, fellows who do not shape my childhood.

But it is Saturday afternoon now, after a movie. I have time to spare before the Parkside arrives in front of Woolworth's. Past the sweet and heavy smell of the counters filled with candies, I walk downstairs to the toy department. I am not there long when two men in suits appear. One is quite ordinary looking, but the other is tall, stocky and darkly tanned. I am wary when they approach. The first man introduces himself as being with the Atlanta Braves and points to the large man, standing hesitantly a few feet away, and asks if I know who the man is. I shake my head, no. The man tells me that this is Joe Torre, the Braves' catcher, and calls Joe Torre over to shake my hand. This is all obviously painful for Mr. Torre, who only shakes my hand and says, "Hello." I say hello. My continued wariness is my only emotion. Then, somewhat dejected, the men leave. I feel that my not knowing who Joe Torre is has wounded, perhaps, his self-esteem, and I feel puzzled and a little sad with the thought that an Atlanta Brave may need recognition from a kid in a Woolworth's five-and-dime. At the time, Joe Torre would have been about twenty-four and a National League All-Star.

When the 20 Parkside arrives, I climb the three steps to the driver, drop my token into the tall, glass cylinder and take my seat near the back of the bus with its few white folks and many black folks, and I must be thinking about Joe Torre, that dark foreigner, who seemed so apart from the normal-looking man—Joe Torre, who is of course only from Brooklyn.

At the east end of Broughton, the bus turns south, past scattered industrial sites and modest residential neighborhoods, arriving again at Victory Drive, crossing over to Paulsen, then to 49th Street down to Waters continuing up 49th, turning at Ash, returning me to 50th. There, with the slow squeak of brakes and a long hiss, the bus doors open. I will wait at the corner for the bus to drive on, leaving behind a puff of cloud and scent of diesel. My house is three doors down, between Ash and Hickory.

LIFE ON A DOUBLE DIRT ROAD AND TWO DEAD ENDS

That's East 55th and Hickory Streets

Jimmy Hill and his sister, Katharine Hill Ruse, grew up near Savannah's Parkside neighborhood in the 1950s, '60s and '70s, but they're pretty certain that their block wasn't considered Parkside. Jimmy and Katharine, along with their younger sisters, Helen Hill Waters and Mary Anne Hill, lived on the corner of east 55th and Hickory Streets. "Ours was the only block [in the neighborhood] with a dirt road in both directions and a double dead end," said Katharine, who lives in Atlanta. "Both distinctions provided unique opportunities not experienced by those kids growing up on pavement and networks of connecting roadways."

Jimmy and Katharine's parents moved to the 1500 block of East 55th Street in 1956, when Jimmy was four and Katharine was two. The Hill family soon welcomed two younger sisters, and as the children grew, they were allowed to venture outside the neighborhood.

Jimmy, who lives in Washington, D.C., explained:

> *It was a different time. My parents, of course, wanted to know where I was going but I was allowed to go anywhere between our home and Daffin Park. They didn't want me crossing Waters Avenue, which always had a lot of traffic. I didn't (most of the time). I remember playing football with* [my friend] *Mark Thomas on Live Oak Street near his home on 50th Street. Not much traffic on Live Oak, but I learned the hard way not to dive after a football on a paved road!*

Jimmy Hill, Helen Hill Waters and Katharine Hill Ruse as happy-go-lucky children on east 55th Street. *Courtesy of the Hill family.*

Closer to home, Katharine remembers Friday evenings and the smell of fish frying because "most of our neighborhood was Catholic."

Neighbors included the Richard Powers family—Mr. and Mrs. Powers and their four daughters, Elizabeth P. Ware, Loretta, Kathleen and Nora. The Myatts also lived on the block. "Mr. Myatt was a city alderman," Katharine said. "I always thought it was funny that we weren't supposed to have fireworks, but he always had them and would give us sidewalk poppers.

"The annual Fourth of July block party always was hosted by Mr. and Mrs. Earl Holden, Katharine said. "They had the prettiest yard in the neighborhood," she added. Jimmy recalls the party being held "under a big tree."

Another large tree was in the center of the 1500 block of 55th and stood directly in front of the Myatts' house. A perfect hill for bike riding was in the 1400 block, Jimmy said. "Once [Katharine] and I were riding our bikes down the hill and she ran smack into a parked car. I thought I would never stop laughing."

Katharine remembers the incident well. "Yes, the hill was awesome. We rode bikes down it without hands. That's how I hit the parked car. I looked at Jimmy and wham!"

The dirt roads afforded plenty of opportunities for games such as drawing houses with sticks and playing half rubber. A patch of woods was between the Hills' house and the Casey Canal, and Jimmy "rambled all through them."

An incident involving a robber in the woods stands out in Katharine's memory. "The police came and scoured the area. It was exciting and scary because we had woods all the way down our side of the street and from there through our backyards were paths connecting all." Somehow the robber escaped, perhaps by crossing the pipes over the Casey Canal, she surmised. The neighborhood boys weren't scared to walk across the pipes, Katharine said. "I did it only once," she added. "I was terrified and lucky that I made it across without falling into that sewage pit."

Katharine and Jimmy agree that their childhood was pretty special. "The degree of freedom to roam the neighborhood was amazing compared to how children are raised today," Jimmy said.

SOUTH GARDENS

Alphabet Streets and Toady Frog Houses

Linda Akins Dooley grew up in the 1940s and '50s in the South Gardens neighborhood, an area east of Waters Avenue and north of DeRenne Avenue, which she remembers as a skinny dirt road. In fact, all of the streets in her stomping grounds were dirt and were lettered A through G. "We lived on F Street, which is now East 71st Street," she said. "Being dirt, F Street was our playground."

A dirt road was a magical place to play hopscotch, jacks and marbles. But Linda's favorite activity seemed to be building what she called "toady frog houses." In the evenings, her mother and daddy sat on the front porch and visited with the neighbors while the children played.

"We had a front porch swing where we spent many hours singing 'She'll Be Comin' 'Round the Mountain' and 'Billy Boy,'" she added.

Linda's father bought the lot next door so he and her mother could plant a garden. However, Linda and her sisters and neighborhood pals had other plans. "We used it as a ball field and a place to play chase through the cornstalks," she recalled. When the old houses were sold at Hunter Air Force Base (as it was known then), Linda's father bought one and had it moved to the garden lot for rental.

Neighbors included the Akinses, who attended South Gardens Baptist Church on D Street. Sometimes Linda's mother allowed her and her sisters to walk to B Street to trade comic books with Betty Jean Brown, Linda said.

The Nunnallys owned a small grocery store on the corner of Waters and A Street. "They would let Mama charge groceries and would even deliver

From left: Shelby, J.P. Akins, Patsy and Reta Akins. The two little girls in front are Nell and Linda Akins Dooley. *Courtesy of Linda A. Dooley.*

them," Linda said. "Mr. and Mrs. Cope ran an even smaller store on our corner. Sometimes we were allowed to walk there and buy a piece of candy or a pickle in a small brown paper bag."

When Mr. and Mrs. Echols opened a drugstore (and sold cherry Cokes with straws), Linda thought she had "moved to town."

FAIRWAY OAKS

Knitting, Cooking and Entertaining Friends

Jan Peterson Coffee grew up in Fairway Oaks, a subdivision developed in the 1950s just south of DeRenne Avenue. One of the streets in the neighborhood overlooks a couple of holes at the Bacon Park Golf Course—hence the name Fairway Oaks.

Jan and her family moved to Fairway Oaks in 1954 when she was three months old. The family included Tom and Ruth Peterson, brother Tom and sister Paige. The Petersons lived in a two-story, Savannah gray brick home with columns. The address was 1331 Brightwood, at the corner of Harlan Drive. Jan remembered:

> *I loved our home. I always thought the yard was so big, but now when I ride by I realize I was just little. My father (who was a physician) had a walk-in cooler room and freezer built in the garage so we could store all the food that patients gave him in payment for his care. Most people did not have insurance back then and Daddy would treat anyone even if they could not afford to pay. We ate very well. My mother had two magnolias planted in the front yard shortly after we moved in. I was just an infant when we moved there, but I always remember those two trees as being beautiful and big. Since Daddy did mostly orthopedic surgery, we were not allowed to climb trees or walk fences. This, of course, just made us more careful about when we climbed those magnolias and walked the fence in the backyard. Fortunately, we never fell.*

Tom Peterson with his sisters, Paige and Jan. *Courtesy of Jan P. Coffee.*

The Petersons' across-the-street neighbors were the Waldherrs, who were European. "Paula and Joe, as they were known to us, did not have any children and were always so kind," Jan said. "They only had one car and Paula never learned to drive. Joe would take the car to work in the mornings and Paula would make a daily walk to Byrd Brothers Grocery on Waters Avenue."

Paula taught Jan and Paige how to knit and make crepes. "We would knit booties, which we proudly wore in the winter," Jan said. Dr. Peterson encouraged Paula to teach Jan and Paige how to cook dishes that were uncommon in the Peterson household.

"Paula only bought Jewish rye bread, and a favorite treat while we were visiting was a sandwich made with strawberry jam and butter on rye bread," Jan said. "To this day, that is a favorite food memory of mine. Joe had a boat and a place on the Forrest River, so he would entertain us on summer days with crabbing and inner tubing."

In those years, Fairway Oaks was bustling with children around Jan's age. "There was always someone to play with if you stepped out of the house," she said. "Paige is two years older than me and our best friends were Nancy and Janet Barber and Christy Hazel."

Jan and her playmates had rules about where they were not allowed to go, including the nearby Casey Canal and the ditches that led to the canal.

"Naturally, those were the most interesting places, and we frequented them whenever we thought we could not be discovered," she said. "We just loved to see what creatures were in the canal."

A pedestrian bridge over the canal connected Fairway Oaks and Magnolia Park. In the summer, Jan and most of the other children were allowed to cross the bridge to go to the Bacon Park swimming pool.

Dr. and Mrs. Peterson routinely entertained friends who mostly lived nearby, but the Chisholms from the Petersons' former neighborhood on 56th also came over frequently, Jan said.

> *Every Monday evening for many years, Mama, Charlotte Henderson, Paula Waldherr and Lavinia Chisholm would play bridge in the living room. Most of the time the husbands would come as well and converse with each other while the women played cards. Daddy would prepare some fantastic dessert and they would drink coffee or iced tea if the weather was warm. When summer rolled around, our screened porch was the venue, and instead of cards, all would gather and shell peas while Daddy would entertain the group with tales from medical school or other adventures. I mainly remember how happy we all were. What an eclectic group of friends—a doctor, two engineers, a widow (who was the only mother I knew who had a job) and two housewives. They were very different people, with diverse backgrounds who enjoyed each other's company so much that they took summer vacations together.*

Often on hot summer nights, Paige and Jan would "drift off to sleep in our upstairs bedroom with the laughter of our parents and their friends as a welcomed lullaby."

DR. PETE'S IS TRIBUTE TO DR. DAD

A Personal Note from Polly

Jan Coffee was blessed to have a loving father, to whom she pays tribute not just on Father's Day, but every day in a business she started twenty-four years ago. Jan and her husband, Joel, own Dr. Pete's, a line of marinades, sauces, salad dressings and sweet baking mixes such as key lime, lemon and cinnamon oatmeal squares.

Dr. Pete was the late Dr. Tom Peterson, who died in 1976. Jan describes her father as a "larger-than-life character" who is remembered by his friends and family as someone who loved to cook and entertain. "He always said he did not want to become a boring doctor who only knew and talked about medicine, so he let his love for great food become a hobby," Jan said. "He grew up enjoying the food of rural south Georgia but always had a penchant for fancier things about which he read and heard."

At his Fairway Oaks home, it was not uncommon for Dr. Peterson to fix lobster tails, beef Wellington and saffron rice for his wife's birthday dinner. "He served my mother breakfast in bed with a single pink sweetheart rose in a silver bud vase most mornings while we were growing up," Jan said. "It was this servant's heart that I so fondly remember about my father. He wanted to help his patients live a better life, honor his wife daily and teach his children to obey God and our parents."

Jan was twenty-two when her father died and twenty-five when she married Joel. "While my husband never knew my father, he had heard about him from the day we first met," she said. "Joel knew about [Daddy's] love of his patients."

Some of Dr. Pete's patients were friends who sat at the Petersons' kitchen table and ate while listening to his "tall tales," Jan recalled. In 1985, when Joel was

Dr. Tom Peterson and his children in front of their Fairway Oaks home.
Courtesy of Jan P. Coffee.

faced with a job transfer to Long Island, New York, he and Jan decided to try marketing Dr. Peterson's recipes. "We named the company Dr. Pete's and have tried to maintain a simple philosophy of creating products that taste as good as if you made them yourself," she said.

When the business first got off the ground, Jan and Joel started with her father's recipe for Burgundy marinade. "We now have about twelve other sauces for grilling and cooking," she said. With the latest addition of Dr. Pete's baking mixes, "you can make an entire meal using Dr. Pete's products, from appetizer to main dish, side vegetables to desserts."

Jan remembers her growing-up years as "wonderful." She had a "loving father" who left her with the "inspiration to follow in his footsteps. Not as a doctor, but by creating a family business that I hope helps others enjoy great meals and the time spent preparing them with their own family and friends."

GREENVIEW

Treehouses, Lemonade Stands and Sam the Dog

When Nancy Heffernan was seven, her parents built a home on Sweetbriar Circle in a cozy neighborhood called Greenview, which is somewhat of an extension of the Fairway Oaks subdivision off Waters Avenue near DeRenne Avenue.

Nancy remembers being blessed with her own room and a "pink-tiled bath and a porch" that overlooked the Municipal Golf Course. "I thought I'd arrived, pretending that all this land belonged to me," she said. "My four brothers—Joe, Mark, John and Gregory—were in heaven with so much to explore." Nancy and her brothers could hardly wait to get home every afternoon from St. James Catholic School to go exploring.

Nancy soon discovered that there were very few girls in her neighborhood, so she "began the interesting mission of becoming a tomboy," she said, adding that she and her brothers wandered around the golf course with the family dogs to learn the lay of the land.

"We could walk all the way to [Benedictine Military School] through nothing but woods, crossing creeks, climbing trees and visiting the [plant] nursery that used to be on Waters Avenue."

Nancy remembers selling lemonade at the eleventh tee on the golf course, which was practically in her backyard. "My famous dog Sam assisted me," she said. "I'd been training Sam for a year to fetch, sit, stay and come." At about one thousand yards, Nancy could command Sam to "sit and stay" while she walked away from him for more than fifteen minutes. "He was one smart English setter," she said.

During lulls at the lemonade stand, Nancy and Sam began a golf ball business. "For about two months we sold golf balls," she said. "Sam would fetch from tee-off two links away and we would sell them for twenty-five cents...sometimes, we sold the golfers their own golf balls twice."

Eventually, it got to the point that Sam would just go get the ball and fetch it for Nancy without her asking. This became such a problem that the golf pro posted a lookout for the setter that had become a hazard to golfers near the tenth, eleventh and twelfth holes, she said. "The enterprise had to end, but it was hard to un-train Sam from fetching golf balls for his own pleasure," Nancy said. "I'd created a monster, and I sure got in trouble for it!"

Nancy and her brothers and their friends explored every day. The nearby Casey Canal was especially interesting. "The boys built rafts and launched them in high waters during the rainy season," she recalled. "Every day after school, I took Sam to the canal. One day, my brother Joe and I found a fourteen-inch alligator."

With Sam's help, Nancy and Joe spent all afternoon trying to capture the gator. "Sam kept the critter corralled while Joe ran to get rope and call in backup," Nancy said. "It was a major operation at age twelve. It took five of us—me, Joe, Mark, some other kid and good ole Sam." They wrapped up the alligator's mouth and took it home and put it in their parents' bathtub, where it stayed for three days.

"That's all mother could stand," Nancy said. "The release was interesting because the gator just seemed to have become our friend by then. We thought he was smiling at us the whole time. We all, including Sam, hated to see him go." Another Heffernan specialty was treehouses. "We specialized in this from the start, since climbing trees was our forte," Nancy said. "We became masters of shovels, axes and world-class construction both below ground and up high. My brothers and other boys from the neighborhood spent an inordinate amount time hiding their efforts from me, but I always found them. "

While Nancy was reading *Nancy Drew* mysteries, her brothers and their friends were making underground forts topped with old bedsprings. These architectural wonders included vented fireplaces and dirt shelves in the walls for candles. "Their finest achievement was a three-story treehouse, with a trapdoor, plywood floors, railings and roped buckets for bringing things up."

Naturally, the boys tried to hide the treehouse from Nancy. Sam, however, wouldn't stand for it. "We found the tree house in one day," Nancy said. "Sam put his nose down and just walked me right up to it, over the canal—hill and dale—to the woods behind BC [Benedictine Military School]," she said. "The boys were so mad that after all their efforts, a *girl* had found it, they felt compelled to abandon the place. It then became a *girl* fort. It was a great place, quite tucked away and wrapped up in a gigantic magnolia tree. When you got all the way up, you could see over the pines as if you were a bird. I had many dreams of flying over treetops after that."

While Nancy took girlfriends up to the treehouse, Sam would patiently wait at the bottom of the tree. As plush as the fort was, it wasn't easy to access. "You had to climb a bit but then, suddenly, you were comfortable," she explained. "Getting down was really scary, so I finally built a retractable ladder—my sole contribution to the fort. My best friend, JoAnn Miles, and I used to love going there until she fell into the canal and came home all wet in the cold and came down with a terrible case of asthma. Her mother wouldn't let her play in the woods much after that."

Instead, Mrs. Miles encouraged JoAnn and Nancy to go to the library, where they became puppeteers for children's groups. "Somehow this led to learning how to make our own clothes, and we quickly became marvelous fashion designers, just in time for puberty," she added.

JoAnn's mother was determined that we learn "ladylike ways" and staged tea parties at her house. "At my house we threw golf balls in the pool for Sam to fetch. Sometimes, we'd steal out of the house late at night to walk the golf course in the moonlight in our peignoir sets with Sam by our side."

One day, Nancy went to the treehouse and it was gone. Years later, it took her forever to find the tree because most of the paths were gone and fences had gone up, separating neighborhoods. "I don't know how it happened so fast, but before I knew it, I didn't want to climb trees anymore," Nancy said, adding that she'll never forget those days on the golf course with Sam.

BONNA BELLA

Foxholes, Rope Swings and Seaboard Sadie

In the early 1960s, Arthur Roberts and Rick Ross spent many a "happy day" wading in the canal at the western edge of what is now the grounds of Savannah Christian Middle School on DeRenne Avenue. "The western edge makes it sound like it was via the Oregon Trail, but it was only one hundred yards from our house on Hughes Avenue," explained Arthur, who now lives in Atlanta. "There was little in the canal but minnows and crawfish, so whatever turned up in the net was a trophy. I felt like Marlin Perkins of television's *Wild Kingdom*."

Between the canal and the backyard, Arthur and his buddy Gus Moore dug a foxhole "bachelors' pad" roofed with saplings and pine straw. "For two ten-year-olds, it was like Club Med," he said. "As seventh graders, we would later meet there to smoke the occasional Salem filched from Gus's mother, rest her soul."

Another popular spot was the rope swing in the woods at LaRoche and DeRenne Avenues that was put up by some of the "big" kids, Arthur said. He explained,

> *One could climb up the trunk six or eight feet to the palm of what was a big live oak hand, and swing out in a continuing physics exercise. On the back swing, your pals would leap on the rope with you, in a maneuver called the "hobo." The extra weight would add speed to the next arc out. The process would be repeated by the next kid waiting in the tree until the knotted end*

of the rope became a knot of kids, laughing like hyenas at the edge, and groaning under the weight in the middle.

Bicycles figured prominently in the lifestyle back then, Arthur said. "No tanks, lights or streamers for us," he added. "Fenders were optional." The best spot for riding were the dirt trails between Bacon Park Drive and what is now the Bacon Park Tennis Center.

They were called the Airplane Trails, partly because the open field which became the Tennis Center was where the model airplane types used to fly their string-controlled planes on the weekends, and partly because if you rode the trails hard enough, it was like flying. With the proper combination

Arthur Roberts with his baby sister, Susan, and their mother, Betty.
Courtesy of Mr. and Mrs. Harrell Roberts.

of speed, abandon and obstacles, one usually did wind up airborne. I never figured out why there was such topographic relief in that plot of land. There were ditches and berms one didn't see in flatland Savannah.

The "ultimate" adventure for Arthur and his pals was sneaking onto Butler's Bamboo Farm, where they would cut a piece of timber bamboo to pole-vault the canal near LaRoche and Bonnie Drive. "Mr. Butler's place was about halfway between us and Savannah State [University], and he guarded it with storied determination," Arthur said. "The stories of his detection and ejection of marauders almost always included a shotgun and near misses of a) rock salt, b) bird shot or—if the teller was on a roll—c) buckshot. Everybody always had a pole, nobody ever got shot, but it was always really close."

With "certainty," Rick says he can "corroborate" much of what Arthur said in reference to Mr. Butler but the events that stick in his mind the most prominently involved "one Seaboard Sadie." Rick explained:

Our entire neighborhood was once part of Ms. Sadie Johnson's property. I believe the area now extends from LaRoche to about two streets west. Seaboard Sadie (who worked for the railroad at some time or other) looked to be older than Methuselah from the first day I saw her. She lived in an old clapboard house which hadn't seen paint for decades. The younger kids in the neighborhood were convinced she was a witch and wouldn't go near the place.

One afternoon, Rick and several of his friends were playing at the edge of the woods bordering the Johnson property. "Suddenly, we heard this shrieking voice commanding us to 'Get up here!'" Rick recalled. "There, to our terror, was the old crone herself, and all but the oldest of us hit the dirt. The oldest kid went up to where she was standing and after a few moments returned with a box of Whitman's Sampler candy. After that, we referred to Seaboard Sadie as 'Aunt Sadie.'"

Because Rick and his buddies were a lot less hesitant to avoid Sadie after the candy episode, every time she called, they pushed and shoved to get to her first.

She would give us handfuls of pennies that she must have been saving for years, because I still have Indian head pennies from as early as the turn of the century—that would be the twentieth century. Although the mantle of

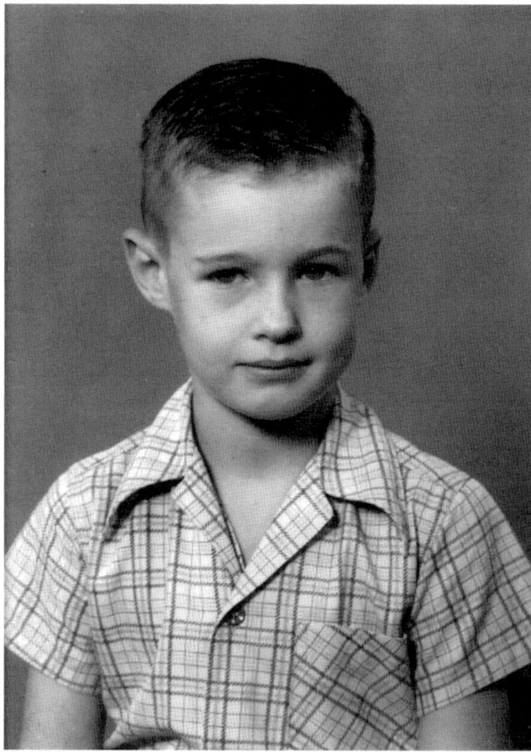

Rick Ross in his younger days. *Courtesy of Rick Ross.*

> *"witch" was pretty much blown by her benevolence, trick-or-treating at Aunt Sadie's was still an event one had to steel oneself for. The house was old, it creaked, it was dark and Aunt Sadie's voice still sounded like a wounded animal. She had a large, oak dining room table and she positioned herself on the far side with a bag of those oversized, orange marshmallow peanuts. With the kids arranged around the table, Aunt Sadie would shove one of those virtually inedible treats at each one in turn with a squawking, "One for you…and one for you!"*

Although both Rick and Arthur are now businessmen on the northern side of fifty-five, they still treasure those neighborhood memories.

ISLE OF HOPE

Wymberley Home Was a Haven for Animals

Teresa Shuman Lockett's childhood home at 11 Colonel Estill Drive at Isle of Hope could have been a zoo, considering all the animals the family adopted through the years. "My father—Ellis Shuman—loved animals," Teresa said. "He would bring home anything that was hurt, hungry or abandoned. These are just a few of the animals we had for pets at our Wymberley home," she recalled, listing ducks, alligators (baby ones that her father found in a Rincon fishing pond), rabbits, mice, raccoons, gerbils, a snapping turtle, dogs, cats, chickens and an opossum that he found by the side of the road. Teresa's dog, Frisky, would spot the opossum about 3:00 a.m. and "go crazy" barking, she said. "My dad would go out in the backyard in his underwear and squirt that [possum] with the hose," she said. One Easter, Teresa found two baby chicks in her basket. "They grew up to be roosters and we had to get rid of them because they would crow at 6:00 a.m. and wake up all the neighbors," she said.

For a mere ten dollars a month, Teresa boarded her horse—a brown and white pinto named Apache—at Byrd's Cookie Shanty on Norwood Avenue. In the 1970s, Teresa was a member of the Rocking S Riding Club. "The big white ring used to sit where the Truman parkway comes into Montgomery Crossroad," she said. Because Teresa didn't have a horse trailer, she would ride Apache from Norwood Avenue to the ring. "My dad would leave his truck there so I would have a place to tie up my horse," she said. "He would bring his bike and ride his bike home." Soon, Teresa's riding route changed because the horse was moved to "Poppell's place" on the corner of Eisenhower Drive and Waters Avenue. She would ride east on Eisenhower, take a right on Sallie Mood, cut through and around Lake Mayer to get to the Rocking S.

When not riding horses, Teresa found plenty to do at the home that she shared with her family—and the numerous animals. "Both the front and backyards were "manicured to a T because my dad worked like a dog to keep it that way," she said. She especially remembers a Japanese maple—"the ones with the big purple flowers that bloom in February"—and a huge oak tree

Mary Glover stands beside Teresa Shuman Lockett, who is on her horse, Apache, in front of Teresa's Isle of Hope home. *Courtesy of Teresa Shuman Lockett.*

that her father hung a rope swing from so that she and her friends could swing out over the ditch by the road. The backyard was beautiful because the entire fence was lined with rosebushes, she said. "My dad used the manure from the horse to fertilize them," she said. "There were gourds hanging from a pole way up high and a birdfeeder hanging from a pecan tree that my parents planted. We had beautiful azaleas all around our yard."

Teresa's favorite spot was on the trampoline in the middle of the yard. "Kids from all over the neighborhood would come over and jump on it, but only after their parents signed a permission slip that my mom typed up and dispersed to any kid that wanted to jump, releasing her from any obligation if someone got hurt," Teresa explained. Some of the friends who enjoyed the trampoline were Kelly Poythress, Mary, Caroline and Harold Glover, Dori Dixon and Kevin and Keith Hohnerlein.

Also in the backyard was a large greenhouse where Teresa's mother often would work until 11:00 p.m. "She would sell plants—begonias, colias, impatiens, ferns and geraniums that she rooted and grew—at the flea market at the old drive-in on Montgomery Street. I went a few times but it was so hot and boring. My mom sometimes would make $200 on a Saturday or Sunday."

Teresa dearly loved crab boils at the Wymberley Yacht Club. "That's what it's called but there were no yachts," she said. She remembers swimming around the dock and shrimp slipping into her bathing suit and "sticking me like crazy."

"It was a big deal to swim to the buoy in the middle of the river," she added. "It seemed soooo far and only the bravest would do it. I don't think I ever did."

During the summer and on weekends, she and the neighborhood kids played hide-and-seek until eleven o'clock at night. "We used the whole street," she explained. "There must have been ten or eleven kids sometimes. We never had to worry being late in this neighborhood." Teresa and her biking pals would peddle all over the island with Frisky trotting along beside.

"My mom was secretary at Isle of Hope Elementary School, so if I ever got in trouble in class, they knew where to send me," she said. "You didn't want to face Montene Swann (the principal) or my mom (who really was sweet)."

In 1992, Ellis Shuman, who was sixty-six, underwent his third open-heart surgery at Memorial. "I had to leave his side and go to Macon to take my nursing boards for two days. When I got back we had to make the decision to take him off the ventilator. He died the next day—February 7, 1992."

SANDFLY'S PEANUT MAN SHELLS OUT WISDOM AND LOVE

A Personal Note from Polly

With an ear-to-ear grin stretching across his kind face, Wesley Phillips comes bounding down the steps of the small bungalow at Varnedoe Drive and Montgomery Crossroad. "What can I do for you today?" he enthusiastically asks a potential customer.

To some passersby, Wesley may be known as the peanut man, but to those regulars who stop at his stand near Memorial Stadium, Wesley is a philosopher and somewhat of a therapist. "If I can wake up in the morning and make somebody smile, that's my medication," he explained, simply. "I remember one man who had a lot of problems. After we talked he told me that he felt 100 percent better."

Wesley began cultivating a positive attitude early on, while growing up in Sandfly. "I've been that way all my life. You never lose it if you keep it going. Even though I may be tired or feeling bad, I never show it. I try to keep a smile on my face."

Wesley grew up here but moved away from Savannah when he finished school. "When we're young we want to have opportunities," he explained. "The opportunities at that time were a little lean." Wesley settled in New Jersey, raised three daughters and retired. He and his wife returned to Sandfly in 1994.

The peanut stand came to pass when he was looking for a way to occupy his two nephews, "little Wesley" and his brother. "I opened this up for them," he said, showing off a simple table on which stand two large cooking pots full to the brim with boiled peanuts. "The peanuts were so good the customers asked us not to close. People just love them."

Wesley also makes and sells wooden picnic tables, but peanuts seem to be his love. "The best in Georgia, that's what I call my peanuts," he said. And what's

Wesley and Mary Phillips alongside their Sandfly peanut stand. *Author's collection.*

his secret? The ever-present grin works its way into a sly smile. "Oh, I can't tell my secrets," he said, laughing. "But I wash them good," he said. "Cleanliness is next to Godliness."

Being at a busy intersection like it is, Wesley's peanut stand gets a lot of exposure. Drivers constantly honk and wave at the friendly fellow conducting business under the beach umbrella. "A lot of young kids stop by to say hi," Wesley said, putting on his imaginary philosopher's cap. "We underestimate young adults and teenagers. It all comes down to how you project things and the tone you use. I try to inject something into their minds to give them something to think about." Children need true supervision, he continued. "My definition of that is fairness, firmness and consistency. If you do that you've got it made. But if you keep letting things slide, it's no good. Their wheels begin to turn."

At that moment, a bus stopped across the street and two women hopped off. "Regular or spicy?" Wesley asked, stirring the pots. "Here, try some of my girlfriends," he said, referring to the nickname he's given his spicy ones.

Two more customers sold. A bag of peanuts and a cup of kindness—it's quite a combination at Wesley Phillips's peanut stand.

A couple of years after this column ran in the Morning News, *I updated readers on Wesley.*

Lately, Wesley has been missing in action, and a caller to the Morning News*'s Vox Populi wondered why. Wesley has been out of sight for several reasons. He and his wife, Mary, went up north for a while to look after one of their daughters who was sick.*

On top of everything else, the digging and pounding in front of his house to make way for the Truman Parkway caused his kitchen ceiling to cave in. But that nagging problem is being taken care of, and Wesley and Mary won't have to move. "I don't want to leave my customers," he insists.

As far as peanuts go, Wesley wasn't cooking and selling for a while because he simply couldn't find any good ones. Now his daughter is better and so are the peanuts. "I've got to buy the best for my customers," said Wesley. "I've got some good friends who I love and they love me." While we were talking, one woman drove by, tooted her horn and waved. Wesley said one day the woman brought him dinner from her church.

Obviously, Wesley provides much more than delicious peanuts from his stand shaded by a big patio umbrella. He always has a cheerful, positive outlook on life.

"There are a lot of nice people around," he said. "If you have love, you have to share it."

HUNTER TEEN TOWN

Where Coke Was Poured in a Glass

During the 1950s and '60s, teenagers whose parents were assigned to Hunter Air Force Base spent a good bit of time at a place they called Teen Town, a nightclub, of sorts, where military parents could drop off their kids. Don Lusk remembers Teen Town as a place where you could have a "healthy, safe evening of dancing in your socks to the sounds of Dana and the Vera Flames or Big Daddy-O Mel Mixon spinning your favorite 45s. It was supposed to be only for [military dependents' teens], but if you knew some or were dating one, you could go there," he recalled. Don and his two brothers, including his twin, were dating dependents, so that's how they became members, he said.

Sara Eubanks and Margaret Hoover were in charge of Teen Town. "[Mrs. Eubanks] didn't tolerate fighting, cussing or loud boisterous action," Don said. "At Teen Town, Coke was something you poured in a glass and put a scoop of ice cream in it, crack was in the wall or on the floor and weed was something you pulled out of the yard so the grass could grow. Grass was something you didn't want to grow, as you would have to cut it on Saturday. If you had the opportunity to become a member of this great place, you were blessed," Don said.

Sandra "Sandie" Anderson Snider echoed Don's comments. "I met many great people there and danced until my feet hurt," she said. "I miss those days and love Savannah with all my heart." In 1959, Sandie's father was transferred to Bermuda, where she finished high school. "As wonderful as

These three girls enjoyed the activities sponsored by Hunter Teen Town. *Courtesy of Hunter Teen Town's website.*

[Bermuda] was and as much fun as their teen club was, it just wasn't the same [as Hunter]," she added.

Another former Teen Town fan remembers Donna Hoover Piland and her mother dancing the hula. "Seems like I remember her hips shaking fourteen times a second," he wrote. Donna moved to Savannah from Hawaii when she was twelve. While in Hawaii, she and her mother learned to dance the hula and were asked to give a demonstration at Teen Town.

"The moment I walked through the double doors, I knew I was in a very special place," Donna said. "Everyone was so friendly and Mrs. Eubanks always had a smile and a kind word."

Donna officially became a Teen Town member when she was thirteen. She recalls attending dances where entertainment was provided by such acts as James Brown and the Mighty Sensations and Preacher and the Deacons. "It was a wonderful time in my life," she said.

Linda Ashby Jung was an Air Force brat who spent the third through eleventh grades in Greenville, South Carolina, where she and other military dependents lived close to one another and played together after school. When that Air Force facility closed in the early 1960s, many of those service people were transferred to Hunter in Savannah. "Most of us were spread all over the city," Linda recalled, because their parents bought homes wherever they could. For Linda and many of the other teens, it was their senior year of high school, which meant they had to attend a different school. Linda was tossed into the mix at Jenkins High School and graduated in 1965. She and many other military kids sought refuge on base at Hunter Teen Town, which offered them the opportunity to "see our friends and reunite," Linda explained.

Mary Louise Kearns Stevens has "the greatest memories of that wonderful teenage hangout." She also attended Jenkins and was a member of the class that shared a split session with Savannah High in 1957.

Tim Ward's father was stationed at Hunter from sometime during the '50s until 1964, a time Tim describes as being at the height of the Cold War. "I had no clue the kinds of things he had to do as an officer in the Strategic Air Command and the sacrifices he and the other air crews made during this time," he said. "Little did I know that they were flying all over the world and, at a moment's notice, were asked to attack targets in the Soviet Union. The air crews and their wives lived under very stressful conditions, so the families were very close to each other."

HALCYON BLUFF

Card Games, Fiddler Crabs and Butterfly Nets

Ellen Rollins Davis grew up in Halcyon Bluff, a neighborhood where she spent endless days pursuing plenty of outdoor adventures. The Rollinses moved to Savannah from Macon in 1957 when Ellen's father was transferred with the Central of Georgia Railway. She remembers her first look at Savannah when her father brought her for a visit before he finalized the move. "Abercorn Street ended at DeRenne Avenue where the J.C. Lewis Ford dealership was," she recalled. "Taking a left on DeRenne and a right on Waters Avenue led us to Montgomery Crossroad then to Whitefield Avenue, which was a narrow, two-lane road."

Ellen thought she was going to the ends of the earth when her father pulled into a subdivision called Halcyon Bluff and stopped in front of 1313 Halcyon Drive. "[My parents] joked about buying a house at the 'dropping-off point,'" she recalled. "I thought it was cool to live in a house with an unlucky number."

At the time, Halcyon Bluff was a new neighborhood with only three streets—Halcyon, Vernon Avenue and Crossbrook Place—but the woods behind the Rollinses' house were quickly developed into more homes. "If you could have put a bomb in the dead center of the neighborhood, even after it was built up, it would have landed on our house," she said. "Unlike the peacefulness (as the name Halcyon Bluff implies), it was a lively place, filled with the noise of children playing outdoors. I knew every new kid that moved into the neighborhood—and believe me, there were lots of them!"

Guests lined up for a photo at Ellen Rollins's old maid– and flapper-themed birthday party. *Courtesy of Ellen Rollins Davis.*

As a child, Ellen rode bikes and played games, outside and in. "My favorite indoor playmate was Diane Paddison (now Churchill), who lived a few doors down from me," Ellen recalled. "Her house was the 'Holy Grail' of board games and I was introduced to so many that are still in my repertoire today." One of Ellen's favorite card games was Mille Borne, which Diane and Ellen played for hours.

Diane's parents are Bob and Phillipa Paddison, whom Ellen remembers as "so cool." "They let us sleep in a tent in their backyard on some summer weekends, but we never slept. We were all up all night playing Mille Borne, Monopoly, a bunch of different card games and the like," she said. Frequently, Diane's family hosted foreign exchange students, which afforded Ellen the opportunity to compare cultures with them.

Since part of Halcyon Bluff backed up to the "mighty" Vernon River, Ellen and her friends were lucky enough to be able to catch fiddler crabs right by their mailboxes in the curbside grates. "Bait was unnecessary, as these little urchins would simply climb up a stick we inserted into the depths below," she said. "If you were successful at pulling a few up and

Ellen Rollins (in braids) with three of her Halcyon Bluff playmates.
Courtesy of Ellen Rollins Davis.

onto the stick, you could have races with them, perhaps to the next crack in the curbside."

Outside of "fiddler crabbing," butterfly collecting was Ellen's next favorite outside activity. "My mother made many a butterfly net for my friends using a cut-off broomstick, a wire coat hanger and plenty of netting left over from my two sisters' fine homemade evening gowns, or 'prom dresses,' as we call them now," she said.

As far as indoor play goes, Ellen and her pals put their imaginations to good use often with their baby dolls and Barbies. "You could purchase the original [Barbie] for $3.09 at the United 5&10 in the shopping center at Waters Avenue and Montgomery Crossroad," she said. "My neighborhood friends and I saved money for ours by making and selling potholders for $0.15 each and going door to door in Halcyon Bluff."

One memorable standout of growing up in Halcyon Bluff was Ellen's eleventh birthday party with its theme—old maids (like the card game) and flappers like the Roaring Twenties.

Ellen's network of friends crossed all age boundaries, she said. The Ogletree boys—Billy, Chip and Jamie—lived next door. "They were all younger than me, but I enjoyed spending endless hours at their home, even through college," Ellen said. "Their mother, Emma Jo, was a neighborhood matriarch, and knew of all the comings and goings of us children," she added. "She seemed to have a magic eye out for us—keeping all of us kids in line. I remember when she ran out of her house one summer afternoon and lectured me about playing in the street."

CARING MOTHERS WHO WENT ABOVE AND BEYOND

A Personal Note from Polly

One day as I sat down at my computer to organize my thoughts for my weekly newspaper column, I decided to check my e-mail. I suppose I was hedging because I knew this piece would be difficult to write. A message popped up from a reader named Abby Johnson who wanted to share her thoughts about the death of her beloved neighbor. Abby's timing was perfect, because I was planning to write about the passing of three women who lived in the neighborhood from whence I came.

Take a moment and think back to your old stomping grounds. Remember those neighbors you knew almost as well as your own mother? Did you play in their yard nearly every day of your childhood life—enough that thirty years later you remember which tree stood where? Did those women make it their business to watch out for you and their child, and every other kid in the neighborhood?

Abby Johnson's neighbor was Betty Hagan, a person she described as a "good woman...the kind of neighbor who rarely exists anymore. You could go to her for a cup of sugar, or to help you soothe your crying baby, or even just to talk something through."

A trio of neighborhood women that I remember with great affection is Miriam Bernstein, Phyllis Shoob and Nancy Bright. Mrs. Bernstein was my longtime across-the-street neighbor—a lovely woman, inside and out. A native of Charleston, she had a wonderful Lowcountry/Savannah accent that was melodious to the ear. She remembered my children with thoughtful gifts and often passed along story ideas to me. Once, she jotted a brief note to me on a bank envelope about how she and her husband Beryl enjoyed reading my articles. It meant the world to me.

Mrs. Shoob and her family lived three blocks away. Her daughter, Laura, was part of my childhood circle of friends. Mrs. Shoob was a petite lady who liked

Nancy Bright (top, middle) with her mother, Mary Nichols, and her daughters, Mary Frances Bright Hendrix and Nan Bright Rimedio, in front of the Brights' East 52nd Street home. *Courtesy of Mary Frances B. Hendrix.*

stylish clothes and was a super saleswoman at the Style Shop and Town & Country. Once when I tried to ride my bicycle standing up with no hands and fell, she came running off her porch to see if I was okay.

I probably knew Mrs. Bright the best. From the fifth grade until college, I was at her house practically every day visiting her daughter, my dear friend Mary Frances. Our families had known each other for years. Her brother, Neill, and my brother, Ken, played Little League baseball together. But mine and Mary Frances's friendship didn't click until I was in the fifth grade and she was in the sixth. I was walking down Harmon Street with a Mary Poppins record album tucked under my arm. Something about that scenario made her laugh, which got me giggling. From then on, we were fast friends who laughed often.

I can't count the number of days I parked my unlocked two-wheeler on the sidewalk in front of the Brights' house. I'd knock on the door and their dog, Miss Boo, would begin to howl. The routine was usually the same—Boo would start barking, hop down off the flowered sofa and jump on the red sofa near the front door. Both had sheets covering the corners where Boo liked to lay. Many times, Mrs. Bright would pick up Boo and take the pooch to the "back" of the house, as they called it. Often, Mrs. Bright would sit in the antique rocking chair and read library books while Boo snoozed on the bed.

Mary Frances and the rest of the crowd and I played cards, climbed trees, walked fences, competed in sand castle–building contests in Harmon Street and pounded out lovely tunes like "Chopsticks" on the piano. Sometimes we'd ride with Mrs. Bright to Smith Brothers on Habersham, where she would do her grocery shopping. I was always intrigued by the fact that she had a charge account there, as well as a tab at Red Lariscy's filling station.

In junior high, the Brights' house became the neighborhood hangout. Actually, our friends began congregating on the corner but usually ended up in front of the Brights' house, where we'd laugh and cut up. I suppose we'd be picked up for loitering today. When we became a bit too noisy, Mrs. Bright would raise the window and very politely ask us to quiet down. She was patient and always cheerful. I still remember how sweet her voice sounded when she answered the phone.

Hers was not an easy life. Her husband, Eddie, died when she was forty-eight, and she went to work as a medical receptionist. Mrs. Bright's parents—Minnie and Pop (Mary and Max Nichols)—moved in with Mrs. Bright not too long after Mr. Bright's death. A handful of Mrs. Bright's oldest friends—ladies in her sewing circle—recalled that kindness and generosity ran in her family. Her maternal grandfather was an Episcopal priest who would often take meals and clothing to the poor, they said.

When the Brights' 52nd Street house was sold, Mrs. Bright moved in with her eldest daughter, Nan Rimedio, and her family. As "Mema," she experienced the joy of watching her three eldest grandchildren grow up. Later, when Nan's husband Nick took a job in south Florida, Mrs. Bright moved in with Mary Frances and her husband, Kevin. Her last years were spent enjoying her youngest grandchildren.

Of her neighbor, Abby Johnson said something that would apply to each of the special women in my old neighborhood: "There is nothing I can say to fully capture the spirit and vivacity of this amazing woman. She spread her love around to so many, and yet it was never worn thin…she was loved by so many, and will be sorely missed."

MONTGOMERY

Horses, Pigeons and Family Memories

The late Tony Ryan and his wife, Porter, were house hunting in the late 1950s when they spotted five acres of marsh-front property on Whitefield Avenue. Back then, though, Whitefield was not Whitefield at all but a country road. The Ryans' address was Route 3, Box 651.

"My parents first saw the house on Easter Sunday," said their daughter, Fran Ryan Tuttle. "I remember because I got my frilly Easter dress dirty in the marsh."

The Ryans bought the house in April 1958 for a whopping $19,250. "The payment was $99.29 a month for twenty-five years," Fran said. "[The area] was so 'country' then that we would ride our horses to St. James [Catholic Church] some Sundays," she recalled. "We'd tie them up in back, and after Mass, we would go to Wyndham's store that was on the corner where St. James now stands. Wyndham's was the gas station/butcher shop/convenience store where everyone gathered."

When people asked Fran where she lived, she said, "Out at Montgomery." "We were so isolated that my father put an 'electric eye' by the driveway, which was quite long," she said. "The house wasn't visible from the street so the place would light up like Memorial Stadium when a [headlight] hit the 'eye.' The lights stayed on for five minutes because, and I quote [my father], 'Five minutes is long enough for anyone to get to the front door.'"

From town, the Ryans drove to their house by going south on Waters Avenue, which ended at Montgomery Crossroad. "We then turned left toward St. James, and after the Hayner's Creek Bridge, we turned right onto Route 3 by Wyndham's store," Fran said.

In addition to Wyndham's, Mrs. Ryan shopped at Buckner's on Route 3, where she bought meat. "While Mom shopped, we would watch the butcher (Mr. Buckner)," explained Fran, who remembers drinking Yoo-hoos and eating Byrd's oatmeal cookies that "came in a white paper bag."

The Ryans always had horses, dogs and, at one time, pigeons that lived in a coop by their stable, Fran said. She remembers riding her horse to visit her friend, Carla Lassiter, whose grandparents (the Lebeys) lived nearby. "We would ride all the way down to Camp Strachan and Beaulieu, then go back and swim off the Lebeys' dock or just play in the mud," she said. "We rode with the Rocking S and barrel raced in an arena by Memorial Stadium."

Fran also remembers shooting targets in the marsh with her father's .22 rifles, and Fran insists that she's "so old" that she remembers when Halcyon Bluff had only five houses and Mayfair had four.

"We went to school at Montgomery School on Shipyard Road on double session," she said. "I went to school in the afternoons. Hesse Elementary School was built because the area was growing and opened in the middle of my fifth-grade year."

Neighbors were few and far between. Fran remembers a memorable visit to Mary Van Schaick's house at the end of Montgomery. An adventurous six-year-old, Fran decided to hop in the dumbwaiter from the dining room to the kitchen. "I got stuck and Hampton [Jaudon], who was Mrs. Van Schaick's butler/cook, had to get me out," Fran said.

Montgomery: Still Living on Her Grandfather's Land

Hampton Jaudon and his wife, Annie Bell, were the grandparents of Vaughnette Goode-Walker, who still lives on "ancestral land" at Montgomery that her grandfather purchased in 1954. The Jaudons came to Savannah from Mobley Pond near Sylvania in 1928 when Jaudon was seventeen and his wife was sixteen. "My grandfather followed his oldest brother, Frederick Douglas Jaudon, to the area and my grandmother's family soon followed," Vaughnette explained.

The Jaudons were employed as domestics for various Montgomery residents, she added. "My grandfather worked for Dr. and Mrs. Newell Turner and lived on the premises on Montgomery Road until my mother was in ninth grade. He stayed with the Turner family part time for many years while working full time for Mary Van Schaick, who lived at the end of Montgomery Road, next door to the Turners."

Vaughnette's grandparents had three daughters—Bertha, Annie Bell and Elizabeth. "My mother is Bertha and I was his only grandchild," Vaughnette said. "My grandmother called him 'Daddy,' so all their three children would call him that growing up. It sounded funny to me later on but of course he didn't mind and between them it even sounded like it had grown to be a term of endearment."

Grandpapa was Vaughnette's nickname for her grandfather, "even though he never seemed old...like what children think a grandfather should look like." His 1988 driver's license said that his height was five feet, six inches, Vaughnette said. "I couldn't believe it because even with my six-foot frame, I could never have been taller than my grandpapa because to me he was bigger than life," she added. "He was a very peaceful and kind man, and even twenty years later, people in the Montgomery community still remember him fondly to me."

Hampton and Annie Bell Jaudon. *Courtesy of Vaughnette Goode-Walker.*

While Vaughnette was growing up, she spent weekends and summers with her grandparents at their Montgomery home. Her grandfather, she explained, was her father figure. "I can't ever remember a time he raised his voice to me," she said. "He would just talk things over with me and defend me to my mother and grandmother. Needless to say, he spoiled me while at the same time teaching me life lessons that I still use today. He taught me to treat everyone with love and respect, leading the way by example."

When Vaughnette was eight, her grandfather became a minister at St. Mary's AME Church in East Savannah, creating another "good example" and leadership role for her to follow, she said. Vaughnette remembers how her grandfather drove to Savannah every Thursday, even though it was his day off. He would go to Smith Brothers on Habersham for "Miss Mary," she said. "I smile every time I visit Smith Brothers, now on Skidaway Island, because I wonder what his life would have been like had he not gone 'to town' every Thursday."

One life lesson of many that Vaughnette's grandfather taught her was about the value of land. He told her that "land was important and that we should never sell it, no matter what." Vaughnette's property is an acre and a fourth and is filled with flowers and shrubs. "The property jumps the ditch, a common occurrence in the area," she said. Across the ditch are giant camellias that he planted.

For many years, Vaughnette said her grandfather would "muse about entering [the camellias] in the Savannah Camellia Show." A couple of years ago, she attended the camellia show in her grandfather's honor. "Maybe someday, I'll enter some of his prize camellias," she said. "Of course, he never did probably because of the 'color line' in those days," she said. "But being the man he was, he never would have disclosed that." Vaughnette says that she often reflects on her grandfather's lessons about race, which began with "God loves everyone."

An award-winning writer, Vaughnette is the author of a twelve-part poem called "Going Home." "It turned into many more poems, of course, and one in particular is called the 'Community House,'" she said. "I read it at a Citizens Advocacy event and connected with the Hodge Foundation, which helped to renovate the Montgomery community house, which is called the Turner-Hodge-Young Community Center at Montgomery."

Sarah Mills Hodge turned the first shovel of dirt and donated the land to the "successors" of Robert Young, a well-known community leader, Vaughnette said. "My grandparents were active supporters of the center and I work there today," she said.

WINDSOR FOREST

Crawdads, Bullfrogs and Country Living

When Spencer Wheeler drives through Windsor Forest, he can point out who lived where and in what house. The neighborhood was Spencer's stomping grounds starting at age six in 1960, when he and his family moved into what was described as "an up-and-coming area." Back then, Abercorn Street Extension stopped at Stephenson Avenue and White Bluff Road was two lanes. "In those days, Windsor Forest was like Bloomingdale and Pooler are to Savannah," recalled Spencer, who is an orthopedic surgeon. "It was considered out in the country," he said, adding that Winn-Dixie in the Habersham Shopping Center was the nearest grocery store.

Spencer and buddies like Paul Phillips, Robbie Hendley, Bill Taylor, Mark Reed, Shawn Saunders and countless others climbed the water tower, swam in the lakes and ponds and camped in the woods. "We had the run of the area and owned those woods," Spencer said. "We'd catch crawdads and eat them and catch bullfrogs and keep them as pets." Spencer and his innovative pals also constructed tree forts on Savannah Country Day School property and what was then Sa-Hi Stables where the Country Day stadium is today. A goat acted as a guard, of sorts, Spencer said. "If we got by the goat, we'd ride the horses."

One day when the guys were exploring, they spotted a rise in the ground and discovered that it was an underground still, complete with a trapdoor. "We never told a soul," he said. One thing's for certain, he added, "if you did something wrong, your parents knew before you got home."

The boys also became friends with longtime African American residents who lived on Coffee Bluff Road, some of whom Spencer still keeps in touch with today. Because there was no Windsor Forest Elementary School when

Spencer started first grade, he rode on a bus to White Bluff Elementary. In the third grade, he transferred to the newly opened Windsor Forest Elementary School. He went to Bartlett Junior High while Windsor Forest High School was being constructed. "We were the first group to go to Windsor [High], so we got to vote on the colors and all that stuff. I can still sing the alma mater."

He remembers protesting the public school dress code and the year it flooded from Arlington Road to Windsor Forest High School. Spencer was living in Windsor Forest when Armstrong State College was built and when the LaVida Country Club was constructed. "I would caddy and get paid $1.50 for nine holes and $3.00 for eighteen," he said. On hot summer days, he and his friends set up a lemonade stand on the fifth hole. Spencer also worked as an usher at the Weis Cinema on Largo Drive and was paid $1.00 an hour. His friends often had jobs at Oglethorpe Mall at long-gone places like the Orange Bowl.

After high school, Spencer went to Armstrong and then to pharmacy school at the University of Georgia before entering the Medical College of Georgia. He has traveled the world but still has a warm place in his heart for his old neighborhood. "Windsor Forest was an awesome place to grow up," he added.

WHITEMARSH ISLAND

A Saltwater Swimming Pool but No Pelicans

As a boy on Whitemarsh Island, Walter Schaff dug up Indian pottery and Civil War cannonballs around the mounds on the eastern end of the island. "We called them mounds, but military people called them batteries," he explained.

Walter, who was born in 1930, has lived on Whitemarsh on and off for years and has delved into the island's history for nearly as long. Originally, much of the land on Whitemarsh was owned by T.P. Saffold, who was an investor in the General Oglethorpe Hotel on Wilmington Island, Walter said. "When the hotel failed as a destination hotel, Mr. Saffold sold his Whitemarsh Island properties." Additionally, Percy Sudgen, who was a well-known Savannah surveyor, laid out the Whitemarsh subdivisions.

Walter was born in Savannah and lived at 417 East Bay Street, which was about as far north as you could live in Savannah. "The Irish say that the farther north you live [in a city] the poorer you are," he explained. But Walter's father enjoyed hunting and fishing and longed to have a place on the water.

In the 1920s, Walter's father brought a house to Whitemarsh from Daufuskie Island by barge. "There were four of five [of these houses] on Daufuskie and they were very, very sturdy because the old-timers knew something we didn't know."

Walter's father paid $575 for property at 165 Penrose Drive. "We burned the mortgage in a bowl in the kitchen," he said. "I remember the day the electricity was turned on…it had no indoor plumbing and no well. The outhouse was a 'two-holer,'" he said.

Walter Schaff and his brothers playing in their saltwater swimming pool on Whitemarsh Island. *Courtesy of the Schaff family.*

His father dug a hole and put in a gate so he and his brothers could enjoy a saltwater swimming pool. His mother was an avid reader who spent many hours reading the classics to Walter and his brothers.

Walter remembers a "one-room place" out back where his family would "take in the homeless." The superstitious black cook tied little sacks filled with "eye of the spider and claw of the fiddler" around her neck to ward off evil spirits. She also washed clothes outside by boiling them in a big pot.

Years ago, an unpaved Penrose Drive meant that driving on it could be tricky, he said. "Men would leave in a convoy in the morning," he said. They routinely carried ropes and two-by-fours so they could pull one another out of the mud, he added. The roads improved when "the WPA came here under the direction of [engineer] S.P. Kehoe." The workers dug ditches, improved the drainage and built "little dams."

In those days, Walter and most everyone else referred to the Tybee Road as the "shell road." For fun, Walter would count how many deer would run across the road. (This, of course, was years before the Islands Expressway was built.) In fact, Walter remembers a farm across from the community club (behind the fire station on U.S. Highway 80) that had "huge fields of corn."

The Schaff brothers on Whitemarsh Island. *Courtesy of the Schaff family.*

In those days, "crabs were so plentiful in Richardson Creek, we counted them by the bushel," he said, adding that he frequently saw eagles and marsh hens, which people hunted. "We'd wait on the docks and count the hens," he said. "I can remember getting three hundred hens."

However, Walter didn't see a pelican until he was grown. Pesticides damaged pelican eggs and wiped out the population in the area, he said. "I never saw an otter either," he added.

TURNER'S ROCK—ORIGINALLY A LAND GRANT FROM THE ENGLISH CROWN

A Personal Note from Polly

An article in the March 12, 1937 edition of the Savannah Morning News *described Turner's Rock as "one of the most desirable pieces of waterfront property left undeveloped near Savannah." That was the year seven local residents purchased the five-hundred-acre property—one half from the Investment Company of Savannah and the remaining portion from Judge Arthur W. Solomon. Until 1925, the land, which also was known as Lacey's Island, had been owned by the descendants of Louis Turner, who received a land grant from the English Crown. In 1928, the land was partially developed when the "new" Savannah Yacht Club was organized. But plans fell through with "the bursting of the real estate boom which accompanied the stock market crash," the story said.*

The island was formerly a cotton plantation with "200 acres of high land and 300 acres of marshland," the Morning News *article said. The men who purchased Turner's Rock in 1937 included Julian Space, Malcolm Bell, Frank D. Howden, Maxwell Lippett, Raymond M. Demere, Raymond D. Sullivan and Jack M. Jones.*

Jones's son, Jack, was eleven or twelve when the family moved to Turner's Rock from Ardsley Park. "It was neat, but pretty wild," Jack recalled. "We went shrimping and crabbing and explored the woods." Before his parents trusted him enough to let him go out in a small bateaux, Jack sought out pals on Bradley Point Road. But once he could go out in the boat, Jack would head over to Isle of Hope to see friends.

Jack and his wife, Mimi, live in the family home on the "point" at Turner's Rock, a spot that the Morning News *reporter must have been writing about when*

The Jack Jones family posed for this portrait in front of their Turner's Rock home.
Courtesy of the Jones family.

he said, "The property holds a commanding view of one of the loveliest salt water stretches in the county."

TYBEE ISLAND

"The Beach" Was One Big Neighborhood for Year-round Resident

Charles Cole's first memory of Tybee Island isn't the beach or the lighthouse, but his father, Buster, giving him a haircut outside in the ocean breeze. "I should have been old enough to know better, but as Buster was buzzing my hair with electric clippers, I took a pair of scissors and cut the power cord," said Charles, who is now fifty-four and living in Colorado. "I remember Buster clicking the clippers on and off a couple times before he realized what had happened. I think he was so relieved that I wasn't fried that he gave me a temporary reprieve from getting a haircut. It didn't matter to me that half my head was partially buzzed."

Charles, who is one of four children of the late Buster and Ernie Cole, believes that his parents—whom he always called by their first names—decided to move to Tybee from Savannah to "escape the busy city life for the simple, quiet, small-town life."

"They didn't spend much time at the beach, but they thoroughly enjoyed swimming at the dock on the Back River and going for afternoon bike rides," he said. The other Cole children were Laura, Slade and Frances.

The Coles moved to Tybee into a 2nd Avenue home in 1962, when Strickland's Store near the South End was also the post office, he said. "You had to walk to the back of the store to ask for your mail. A phone call to Savannah was long distance and Tybee phone numbers were only three digits and were handled by a switchboard operator."

Charles Cole. *Courtesy of Charles Cole.*

In 1963, the Coles bought a larger house at the corner of Lovell Avenue and 12th Street. "The first winter was interesting because the house wasn't insulated or adequately heated for cold weather," Charles said. The house also wasn't air-conditioned. "Some days the ocean breeze just wasn't enough to keep you cool." It wasn't until Charles was a teenager that his parents bought a window unit for the kitchen. Buster also had installed a large attic fan that "helped make the hot summer days bearable," he said. "To say Buster was thrifty is an understatement! But the tough economic times this country is experiencing today certainly gives me a greater appreciation for Buster's thriftiness and conservative saving. As a kid, I remember collecting empty Coke bottles around the island and redeeming them for spending money."

Charles attended Tybee Elementary School, which—in retrospect, he said—reminded him of the *Little House on the Prairie* school on television. "Each classroom consisted of two grade levels," he said. As a third grader, Charles remembers having to stay after school and walking home with his teacher. Another major event during Charles's elementary school days was the fire that destroyed the Tybrisa Pavilion.

"The blaze was way too big for Tybee's small volunteer fire department," he said. "I remember seeing fire trucks from other towns helping battle the fire. Since we were up most of the night watching the fire, Ernie let us stay home from school the next day."

Another vivid memory of Charles's involved a storm. "When I was maybe ten years old, Tybee was a potential target for a major hurricane," he said.

"As a kid, the ocean waves seemed huge. It also was fun trying to ride a bike in the high winds. The firemen went cruising around town in the fire truck warning people to evacuate. Buster was at work [with the railroad] and Ernie decided that we would hunker down and stick it out. Fortunately, the hurricane missed. After seeing the devastation caused by major hurricanes like Katrina in recent years, I often ask myself what was Ernie thinking?"

After Tybee School, Charles went to Myers Junior High School. "Instead of taking the long, slow bus ride into town, I decided that hitchhiking a ride was quicker," he said. But catching a ride wasn't always easy. "Tybee was like a ghost town in the winter," he explained. "Many mornings I would stand on the side of the road for ten minutes or longer waiting for a car to pass."

Sometimes, Charles's rides would drop him off on the side of U.S. Highway 80 where the road forks at 80 and the Islands Expressway. There, he would have to hitch another ride and usually was tardy by the time he got to school. "My teachers used to say I was going to be late to my own funeral," he said.

After school, Charles would hitchhike back to Tybee, where he found plenty to do. "It was a great place for a kid to ride a bike," he said. "There were no worries about traffic, and you had the freedom to just ride anywhere on the island. I remember peddling my cool Schwinn to Fort Pulaski with friends. There were no ten-speed or mountain bikes back then. The Lazaretto Creek Bridge seemed so tall. The best part, of course, was racing down from the top."

During the summer, Charles would ride his bike to the old DeSoto Beach Motel swimming pool, where his mother and a friend had organized a swim club. "It was great to be able to hop on your bike during the hot summer and cool off at the pool," he said.

Basketball also was a popular pastime at the Coles'. "Buster and Slade built a court in our backyard," Charles said. It proved to be a magnet for players like Ben Burnsed, Jimmy Brown, Robbie and Joe Powers, Biddie Shaw, Norbert Chandler and Jerry Rogers.

Before he could legally drive, Charles drove an old clunker station wagon around the island with Buster's permission. "In the winter, you usually had the road to yourself unless you happen to pass a Tybee police car," he said. "Fortunately, I never got stopped. Can you picture them asking me for my license and insurance? I think Mayberry is the only other place I could have possibly gotten away with that."

Water-skiing in the Back River was great fun for Charles and Slade. Before either of them could legally drive, Buster would trailer the boat to the boat ramp. "The only problem was that Buster didn't know how to back

Tybee Island has long prided itself on being a family beach, and this mom and her three children attest to that claim. *Courtesy of Mary Frances B. Hendrix.*

up the boat trailer," Charles said. "Slade and I had to unhitch the trailer from the car and push the trailer down the boat ramp by hand. This got a little difficult, especially when he had to roll the trailer down the incline of the boat ramp."

After finally putting the boat in the water, the Cole brothers and their friends would stay in the river for hours and often would experiment with various types of ski equipment. Charles recalled:

> *One time Slade built a ski kite from a kit. The only problem was that our small boat didn't have enough power to lift a skier into the air. We discovered, though, that if we pulled the kite into a strong wind, I could fly because I didn't weigh much. Once I got up, I was terrified. I felt like I had no control and was afraid I was going to crash. I was screaming to be let down but Slade just ignored me. I think that was the only time the kite got any air time.*

Usually it was dark by the time Charles and Slade took the boat out of the water and ate dinner. "We'd then play ping-pong or watch television (all three channels)," Charles said.

Riding to town with Buster wasn't necessarily a treat for Charles. "The old Tybee Road didn't have passing lanes like it does today," Charles explained. "Buster used to be the slowest driver on the road. On a busy summer day, I would want to hide because frustrated drivers couldn't pass us. I never understood why he drove a maximum of forty miles per hour."

"A 1965 Chevy Bel Air station wagon is the family car I remember most," Charles said. "This became my first car when I went off to school at Southern Tech. It had an a/m radio but no air conditioning. The gas gauge was broken, so I would use a wooden yardstick to measure the gas level."